# Reading and Writing American History

*An Introduction to the Historian's Craft*

**Peter Charles Hoffer**
*University of Georgia*

**William W. Stueck**
*University of Georgia*

VOLUME *1*

**D. C. Heath and Company**
*Lexington, Massachusetts    Toronto*

*Address editorial correspondence to:*

D. C. Heath and Company
125 Spring Street
Lexington, MA 02173

Acquisitions Editor: James Miller
Developmental Editor: Lauren Johnson
Production Editor: Bryan Woodhouse
Designer: Alwyn Velásquez
Photo Researcher: Martha Shethar
Production Coordinator: Richard Tonachel
Permissions Editor: Margaret Roll

International Standard Book Number: 0-669-24902-5

10  9  8  7  6  5  4  3  2  1

For Brad Chapin, who taught us all
and William Hull, who loved us all

—P. C. H.

# To the Student

Most of you have purchased *Reading and Writing American History* for use in a survey course in American history. Such surveys were instituted at the end of the nineteenth century with the understanding that college students had to know American history to be fully educated. One hundred years later, American college educators have discarded many of the educational assumptions and policies of the 1890s. Women and men are no longer educated separately, nor do we assume that one gender should be subordinated to another. We have come to understand that African-Americans, Asian Americans, Native Americans, and European Americans can and must learn together on a basis of equality and mutual respect. Fortunately, we still regard history as the centerpiece of a college education, and for good reason.

Whether you are taking this course because it is required or because you have decided to study history as an elective or as a major, history offers the opportunity to learn skills that will follow you throughout your lifetime. History is the study of what people thought and did in the past, but these women and men cannot tell you that story. An old (but true) adage reminds us that in every story there are three elements — the story itself, the storyteller, and the listener. The listener performs by far the hardest task. *Reading and Writing American History* is designed to help you, the listener, understand American history.

*Reading and Writing American History* is not intended to replace your textbook but to be used in conjunction with it. The explanations, readings, and exercises in this book approach history as a way of knowing, a set of skills for making sense of a world that is gone. You cannot go back in time and bring people from the past back to life, but you can use your intelligence and imagination to re-create those different worlds in your own minds. *Reading and Writing American History* was devised to give you the skills to navigate that journey into the past.

This volume is divided into two parts. The first focuses on research skills — for example, how to read a historical document, how to use a textbook, how to find references in the library, and how to understand a map. The second part of the book builds writing proficiency, beginning with outlines and narratives, and continuing on to analytical and biographical skills. Within each chapter, the exercises increase in difficulty, and each skill builds on the last. Throughout the volume, the topics and exercises follow the chronological development of the first half of a survey course.

## Acknowledgments

The final version of *Reading and Writing American History* was a collaborative endeavor. The authors have worked together at every stage of the project; Volume 1 is the work of Peter Hoffer, and Volume 2 is the work of Bill Stueck. The editors and staff of D. C. Heath, in particular Laurie Johnson, James Miller, and Bryan Woodhouse, were stern when they had to be and kind when kindness counted. Their support for the project was unwavering and their suggestions always salutary. Many of our colleagues in the teaching profession also provided incisive and helpful comments. We are grateful for these to J. Lee Annis, Jr., Montgomery College; Betty B. Caroli, Kingsboro Community College; E. Wayne Carp, Pacific Lutheran University; Kathryn J. Carr, Southern Illinois University; William Cecil-Fronsman, Washburn University; David De Leon, Howard University; Jane B. Donegan, Onondaga Community College; Lloyd Farrar, Imperial Valley College; Beverly Garrison-Chism, Oral Roberts University; Wendy F. Hamand-Venet, Eastern Illinois University; Louis Keith Harper, University of Kentucky; Constance M. Jones, Tidewater

Community College; Anne Klejment, University of Saint Thomas; Rita E. Loos, Framingham State University; Cathy D. Matson, University of Delaware; Holly A. Mayer, Duquesne University; Clay McShane, Northeastern University; J. Carroll Moody, Northern Illinois University; Linda M. Papageorge, Kennesaw State College; Louis W. Potts, University of Missouri-Kansas City; Ronald Reitveld, California State University-Fullerton; David L. Rowe, Middle Tennessee State University; Mary Ellen Rowe, Central Missouri State; Dale J. Schmitt, East Tennessee State University; Michelle Simpson, University of Georgia; J. William T. Youngs, Eastern Washington University.

Now *Reading and Writing American History* no longer belongs to its authors or its publisher. It belongs to you. If it is a success — if it helps you to "do" history and enjoy doing it — the credit belongs to more people than just its authors. You deserve recognition as well; your effort and enthusiasm are essential. Good luck and enjoy!

P. C. H.
W. W. S.

# Contents

**9**   BIOGRAPHY: LIFE AND TIMES
*Abraham Lincoln, Frederick Douglass, and Their
Generation*   127

**10**   BIG QUESTIONS: INEVITABILITY,
MORALITY, AND THE LESSONS OF
HISTORY
*Civil War and Reconstruction*   139

# 1 WHAT IS HISTORY, AND WHY SHOULD WE STUDY IT?

## Native Americans and Old World Peoples

In a recent popular song, the singer Madonna prides herself on being a material girl in a material world. There is much truth in what she sings, for everywhere today we are surrounded by evidence of the triumph of technology. "Material Girl" can be seen on videos and heard on CDs, technologies that did not exist a generation ago. The pace of change in our world is so rapid that images and words collapse into "white noise," a discord of sights and sounds that blurs past, present, and future.

The study of history can rescue you from this buzzing confusion, giving you a sense of your place in time. History enables you to recognize the powerful forces that shaped your world and links you to the men and women who made those forces. History teaches you that your lives and aspirations are the culmination of the hopes and fears, the labors and the loves, of people in the past.

### EXERCISE 1: *History in Your Pocket*

As concerned as you are with the present and the future, you are a historian. Take a moment to look through your pockets, wallets, and bags. There you will find evidence that ties you to the past. A sales receipt, a snapshot of your family, a driver's license, your college ID card — all place you in the stream of history. You carry history in your head as well as in your pockets. Memories of old acquaintances, places you have seen, and homes in which you have lived are history you can call forth with a blink of the eye.

Scrutinize the evidence you have found in your pockets and bags. If you were a historian in the future, and you came upon this collection of evidence, what might it tell you about the people who lived during this period? What ideas were important to them? What material things and personal relationships did they value? Think about it.

## *The Meanings of the Word* History

The word *history* has three meanings. First, history is a necessary part of human culture. Every cultural group formulates and expresses in words and images a conception of the origin of the group. Such collective, deeply embedded ideas of the past give the group a sense of identity and coherence. Without history, the group would lose its grasp on reality, just as an individual who forgot his or her past would have amnesia. A people's history also tells individuals what is good and bad, what they must do to survive and prosper, and how to pass their values on to new generations.

Second, history is a substantive body of information that scholars assemble about what people did, thought, felt, and perceived in the past. This collection of facts is sometimes overly compressed in the classroom into mind-numbing lists of names, dates, and places. Such lists are incomplete and misleading because they do not convey the richness, drama, and irony of human endeavor.

Third, history is a way of studying past events, a mental "discipline" in which you sift evidence from surviving sources, fashion facts from evidence, and weave them together into a coherent story. The three main sections of this chapter consider the three domains of history in detail.

## History and Identity

It will be easier to grasp the basic truth that history gives you your identity and values if you mentally transport yourself to a less cluttered and crowded time. Imagine that you are a Pilgrim on the deck of the *Mayflower* in the middle of the Atlantic Ocean in the fall of 1620. It is cold and damp in the hold of the ship, frigid and wet on deck. You can hear the creak of the rigging and the thump of the waves on the hull, the cursing of the sailors, and the cries of the other Pilgrims' children.

In that perilous time and place, you have no trouble understanding your place in history. You are going to the New World to escape religious persecution in Europe. If there had been no wars of religion raging across the face of Europe, there would have been little reason for you to flee. If you survive the voyage, you will find a haven on the far shore because companies of merchants seeking rare minerals and furs have already built trading posts there. Without the rise of commerce and the age of discovery, there would be no companies sending their agents in search of gold and beaver pelts. You will find that shore because navigators developed compasses and because shipbuilders learned how to rig their boats for ocean travel. Standing on the deck of the *Mayflower*, you know how and why you are part of history.

Today, the Pilgrims' survival in the New World is celebrated with the holiday of Thanksgiving, but students of American history should learn another, more important lesson from this handful of determined immigrants. They believed with unshakable faith that a knowledge of history was a vital part of their lives. For them, history was filled with lessons and directions for conduct and belief; it told them what they must do to carry out their mission in the New World.

The Pilgrims were a small group of men and women in the great stream of English-speaking immigrants to the Atlantic shore. In that migration they joined Africans from many nations and several other European peoples, including Dutch, French, German, Irish, Portuguese, Spanish, and Welsh. Some came willingly; others wore chains on their ankles and wrists. Some longed for ease and luxury;

others expected hardship. Waiting on the shore were Native Americans who spoke many dialects and practiced customs as varied as those of the Europeans. All of these peoples relied on written accounts or orally transmitted stories about their past to remind them of who they were and what made them distinct.

The peoples who met on the Atlantic coast of North America in the sixteenth and seventeenth centuries had well-developed views of their origins and a strong sense of their identities. The Native Americans of the northeastern woodlands used songs, stories, and speeches to link the past and the present. These accounts moved back and forth through time, uniting the history of their people with natural events and supernatural forces.

The English-speaking explorers and settlers had a more linear, or straightforward, idea of time that fit their sense of self. English adventurers like Walter Raleigh, the founder of the Roanoke colony, sought personal glory and regarded history as a story of conflicts among great men, clashes that featured the rise of England's power and the submission of its enemies. English Protestant reformers, including the Pilgrims, had a different personal mission — to purify the church of corruption — and saw history as a series of divine verdicts upon human weakness. The Pilgrims' idea of time began with creation and ended with redemption of the saved.

## EXERCISE 2: *What Our Histories Reveal About Us*

Following are an excerpt from an Iroquois folk tale, a reproduction of an Iroquois religious mask, and a selection from the journal of William Bradford, a leading Pilgrim. Each is related to a historical event in the life of its author's people. At the same time, each reveals the way in which its author conceptualizes his people's values and place in history. The introductions, or headnotes, to each piece provide information to help you understand what you are reading. After each are questions for you to answer.

Note that all of these selections record or recall the voice of the original historical figures. The language will thus seem unfamiliar to you. These are called primary sources and we will discuss them further in the next chapter.

Ⓐ The Iroquois Indians in what is now New York State were surrounded by enemies and constantly fought to protect themselves, extend their territory, obtain captives, and maintain their honor. Their longhouses were surrounded by wooden walls, and bands of warriors periodically marched off to raid the villages of their neighbors and rivals, the Algonquin-speaking peoples of New England and Canada.

Raiding was an extension of the hunt for game. Like all hunter-gatherers, the Iroquois believed that they and the animals they hunted shared the world, and only by hunting in certain set ways could that sharing benefit both the Iroquois and the animals. Hunters not only learned how the animals lived but taught themselves to think like the animals. The animals themselves told the Indians when the seasons of the hunt should begin — frogs along the streams signaled the beginning of the fall hunt, for example — and the Iroquois called to the animals of the hunt with song. Woodland lore and Indian custom merged in Native American rituals. After the hunt was over, the Iroquois lovingly returned the animal remains to the forest to ensure that the supply of animals would never diminish.

The warrior–hunter is a predator, and the Iroquois had to learn to control the aggressiveness that raiding and hunting bred. The following Iroquois folk tale explains how the first Indians learned to master their own aggression.

This is a saga concerning the first people — the ancient people — the people of the beginnings — who live now and who lived also when the earth was new, and, therefore, was young. . . .

In the land of the sunrise . . . there was situated a village of these first people. . . . There came a day when one of the young men, "He-Who-Cleaves-the-Sky-in-Twain" resolved to form an expedition to make a raid westward into the distant regions through which pass the daily path of the sun.

So to promote his design [he] induced his friends to prepare a great war feast . . . he announced to the public assembled there his purpose of leading a troop of warriors far into the west . . . to slaughter unknown men and to obtain the scalps of alien peoples as tokens of their prowess and their courage in warfare. In response to this appeal twenty-eight young virile men volunteered to be members of the war party.

As these warriors traveled on they finally reached a place in which they found the habitations of a people whom they did not know, but these unoffending persons they ruthlessly killed and scalped. After this bloody exploit they journeyed westward. . . . These bloody exploits were repeated wherever they found a village of people dwelling on the line of their march. This bloody work continued for many moons.

About this time they fell in with a person, a male man being, whose towering stature reached one-half the height of the tallest trees. [One of the warriors said] "I think that the next move to be made is to decide to kill this man being whom we have met in this place . . . so let us attack him at once."

So deploying they at once began to assault him by shooting their arrows at him, and by striking him with their war clubs and with their stone hatchets; but they could not make any impression on him; they failed to harm him in the least.

At last the strange man being said to them, kindly, "What is that you desire to do? Do you imagine that you can kill me?" Then they answered, "That is, indeed, our purpose, as it has been our design in making our journey hither to kill all persons who might fall in our way, no matter who they might be."

To this frank admission of their purpose to kill him, this strange man being replied, "The purpose for which you are banded together is not good. And from this time forward you must utterly renounce it and strictly desist from carrying it out. It is quite impossible for you to kill me. And I came to meet you here for the purpose of giving you this counsel. I watched you on your way to this place, and I saw with grief that you killed many people. I want you to know that the reason why I came to meet you is that you have now committed wrongs enough on innocent people. And I want you to know that if you will not cease from committing these wrongs you yourselves also shall perish."

Then He-Who-Cleaves-the-Sky-in-Twain replied, saying, "We are very thankful to you for this good counsel, and we will try to abide by it.". . . Then the strange man being merely replied, "Do you then start on your journey." And while they listened to him with bowed heads he vanished from them; they did not know or see whither he went.[1]

1. What motivated He-Who-Cleaves-the-Sky-in-Twain when he set out on his journey? _____

_____

2. What did his warriors regard as proper conduct then? _____

_____

3. To what physical object does the teller of the folk tale compare the mysterious "man being"? _____

_____

4. What does this suggest about the relationship between nature and moral good-

   ness in Iroquois thinking? _____

   _____

5. What did the warriors learn from the man-being, and how did the lesson change

   their concept of themselves? _____

   _____

6. What lessons did the folk tale teach the Iroquois who heard it? _____

   _____

**B** Like their neighbors and rivals among the Native American peoples, the Iroquois believed that the world was filled with spirits. Some of these, like the man-being, were benevolent and taught the Native Americans how to live and prosper. Other spirits were dangerous and malevolent; they had to be placated or fooled, or they would bring death and destruction. Some spirits were animals, and lived in the forests and fields with the Indians. Others were manifestations of the earth, sky, rain, and sun. Sometimes a shaman or medicine man supervised this folk worship, but more often than not a group of men were charged with keeping harmony between the Indians and the spirit world.

During important Indian religious ceremonies, dancers and singers wore masks. For example, the False Face Society of the Iroquois were healers, and their songs and dances had the power to cure the sick. Each of the false faces they wore had its origin and place in Indian folk stories. The face in Figure 1.1 is "Crooked Mouth," who dared to challenge the earth and was bent by an onrushing mountain. The face was carved from a living tree by members of the Onondaga tribe of the Iroquois nation. The eyes are copperplate. The hair is from a horse's tail. Such faces, like the folk tales of the Iroquois, did not capture a particular moment in time but tied past to present, and present to future.

1. How might such a mask play a role in curing a sick person — assuming that the

   sick were afflicted with evil spirits? _____

   _____

2. The carving, care, and use of the mask were restricted by custom to only those individuals who had been initiated into the secrets of the society. How might such men gain power and status from their participation in the healing rites?

   _____

   _____

**C** The Spanish, French, and Dutch had all come to North America to extract the wealth of the Americas and carry it back to Europe. The riches of empire made Spain, France, and the Netherlands powerful states. England entered the race for empire early in the seventeenth century, and its efforts were never as well coordinated as those of its European rivals. The Spanish crown monitored its colonies closely and wrote comprehensive manuals for its colonial viceroys (governors). The French and Dutch colonial companies were also successful enterprises. England's colonies were poorly governed by absentee landlords, milked by badly run companies, and ignored by indifferent monarchs. Ironically, it was this sorry state of affairs that allowed religious zealots who could not practice their faith safely in England to establish their own havens in England's overseas domain.

FIGURE 1.1   "Crooked Mouth" — Iroquois Medicine Mask

The Pilgrims, a small sect of Christian refugees, established just such a colony on the jagged coast of New England and named it after a port city in England — Plymouth. Their leader was William Bradford, and the following excerpt is from the opening pages of his journal describing the Pilgrims' wanderings in search of freedom to worship in their own way. His journal took the form of a diary, in which he recorded great events, personal reflections, and his sense that God had chosen the Pilgrims for a special mission. In the passage he describes the persecution of Protestants in sixteenth- and early-seventeenth-century England, while introducing his sect and hinting at what he believed to be God's plan for the Pilgrims.

It is well known unto the godly and judicious, how ever since the first breaking out of the light of the gospel in our honourable nation of England, (which was the first of nations whom the Lord adorned therewith after the gross darkness of popery [Roman Catholicism] which had covered and overspread the Christian world), what wars and oppositions ever since, Satan hath raised, maintained and continued against the Saints [the Pilgrims] from time to time, in one sort or another. Sometimes by bloody death and cruel torments; other whiles imprisonments, banishments and other hard usages; as being loathe his kingdom should go down, the truth prevail and the churches of God revert to their ancient purity and recover their primitive order, liberty, and beauty.

But when he could not prevail by these means against the main truths of the gospel, but that they began to take root in many places, being watered with the blood of the martyrs and blessed from heaven with a gracious increase; he then began to take him to his ancient stratagems, used of old against the first Christians. That when by the bloody and barbarous persecutions of the heathen emperors he could not stop and subvert the course of the gospel . . . he then began to sow errors, heresies and wonderful dissentions amongst the . . . professors [people] themselves, working upon their pride and ambition, with other corrupt passions incident to all mortal men . . .

When as by the travail and diligence of some godly and zealous preachers, and God's blessing on their labors, as in other places of the land, so in the North parts [of England], many became enlightened by the word of God and had their ignorance and sins discovered unto them, and began by His grace to reform their lives and make conscience of their way, the work of God was no sooner manifest in them but presently they were both scoffed and scorned by the profane multitude . . . Which, notwithstanding, they bore sundry years with much patience. . . .

Yet seeing themselves thus molested, and that there was no hope of their continuance there [in England] by a joint consent [the Pilgrims] resolved to go into the Low Countries [the Netherlands today], where they heard there was freedom of religion for all men. . . .[2]

1. According to Bradford, what was the fate of the first Protestants? _____

    _____

2. Who (or what) was the root of the trouble? _____

    _____

3. How did the Pilgrims become a distinct religious group in England? _____

    _____

4. What persecution did they face there? _____

    _____

5. How did the Pilgrims respond to that persecution? _____

    _____

6. According to Bradford, what motivated their actions throughout; that is, how did they identify themselves as a group? _____

    _____

# Differences and Similarities: Why History Is Two-faced

As the preceding exercise demonstrates, the era of the founding of European colonies in North America differed markedly in many respects from our own. There appear to be similarities as well, but the differences are quite striking, and they lend our study of history much of its excitement. Without assuming some degree of similarity between the past and the present, however, you could never begin to guess the motives of men and women who lived before you. Thinking about the past is like taking a trip to a country whose customs are exotic and intriguing, but some of whose guides speak your language. You enjoy the differences but are reassured by the similarities.

History always faces in two directions. One face looks backward, seeing differences between past and present. History's other face looks directly at you and requires you to re-create the feelings and perceptions behind those very differences. You cannot perceive differences unless you make comparisons and connect the past and present.

Some of the differences between modern life and life in the seventeenth century are so overwhelming precisely because they touched every aspect of daily life. For example, most of us take for granted that we can control light and darkness, heat and cold, with the flick of a switch. In the seventeenth century, the distinction between day and night, warmth and chill, was sharp and beyond the control of many people. The French historian Lucien Febvre was struck by this difference between the modern world and its predecessor:

> What does the contrast between night and day mean to us . . . of the twentieth century? Practically nothing at all. A switch, a movement of the arm, and sunlight gives way to electric light. We are the masters of light and darkness. . . . [But people in the seventeenth century] were not masters of light, especially the poor who did not even have oil-lamps or candles to light when night came on. Their life was divided . . . into day and night, white and black, absolute silence and the noisy bustle of work. . . . Today, there is heating everywhere. . . . Anybody going into [a] house in the [seventeenth century] in January felt the cold . . . the silent dark cold of heatless dwellings. You shivered in anticipation, in the same way as you had been shivering all the time in church. Just as you shivered in the king's palace despite the big fireplace that devoured whole trees. . . . So can we really believe that a life of this sort fashioned in [people] the same mental habits and the same ways of thinking and feeling, the same desires, the same actions and reactions as our own life does in us?[3]

If Professor Febvre was right in claiming that the world of 1600 was so profoundly different from our own that we cannot assume that men and women then felt or did as we do, how could anyone begin to write a history of that time? Febvre was not arguing that it is impossible to know what people did and thought in the past but only that we must always take into account the differences between the modern world and the world 400 years ago — or 50 years ago.

## EXERCISE 3: *Discovering Differences*

Following are three pieces of evidence about customs and thought in seventeenth-century Europe — ways of life that the European settlers brought with them to the New World. Examine the selections and illustration, and ask yourself in what ways people 300 years ago differed from people today. How were they similar? More specific study questions follow each of the passages.

**A** Slavery was not offensive to most seventeenth-century Europeans. Though it did not flourish on the Continent or in the British Isles, slavery was planted in Latin America by the Spanish and Portuguese. They bought men and women captured in war in West Africa and transported them to the Caribbean, Mexico, and Central and South America to work on plantations and in mines alongside the Indians that the Europeans enslaved. To facilitate the African slave trade, the Portuguese, followed by the Spanish, the French, the English, the Dutch, and finally the German and Swedish traders, built forts on the coast of West Africa. As slavery became a fixture of the labor system of the American colonies, the slave trade became more and more lucrative. The European nations engaged in it fought wars to determine which country's traders would control which portions of the West African coast.

Some Christian leaders objected to slavery or sought to curb its worst abuses. Although the medieval theologian Thomas Aquinas believed that slavery was part of the natural order of the world, and later religious thinkers like Martin Luther and John Calvin did not see any contradiction between Christianity and human slavery, other Christians argued that slavery violated the basic precept of human equality that Christianity proclaimed. The following passage is a segment of the reply that a Jesuit teacher in Angola wrote to a Roman Catholic priest in Brazil. The priest, Father Sandoval, was worried that the Africans had been captured illegally. The teacher, Luis Brandaon, countered with legalistic reasons why the priest should not trouble himself with doubts about the slave trade.

Your reverence writes me that you would like to know whether the negroes who are sent to your parts have been legally captured. To this I reply that I think your reverence should have no scruples on this point, because this is a matter which has been questioned by the Board of Conscience in Lisbon, and all its members are learned and conscientious men. . . . Since the traders who bring those negroes [to Brazil] bring them in good faith, those inhabitants [the Portuguese who had plantations in Brazil] can very well buy from such traders without any scruple, and the latter on their part can sell them, for it is a generally accepted opinion that the owner who owns anything in good faith can sell it and that it can be bought. . . . Besides, I found it true indeed, that no negro will ever say he has been captured legally. Therefore your reverence should not ask them whether they have been legally captured or not, because they will always say that they were stolen and captured illegally, in the hope that they will be given their liberty. . . . And to lose so many souls [that is, potential converts to Christianity] as sail from here [as slaves] — out of whom many are saved . . . does not seem to be doing much service to God.[4]

1. To what authority does the teacher refer the priest? _____

_____

2. Is it scriptural? _____

_____

3. What three arguments does the teacher offer the priest to quiet the latter's doubts

about the legality of slavery? _____

_____

4. Does the teacher's letter hint at any underlying economic reason why the slave

trade should continue uninterrupted? _____

_____

5. How does the teacher's view of slavery differ from that held by modern men

and women? _____

_____

**B** In the first half of the seventeenth century, London was a study in motion and contrast: the homes of the wealthy stood next to the hovels of the poor; bustling businesses and shops abutted pestholes and "rookeries" of crime. Periodically, epidemics of smallpox, bubonic plague, and tuberculosis swept off whole neighborhoods of people, but fire was the worst danger. In 1666 much of the housing shown in Figure 1.2 was destroyed by a great fire. Such conditions prompted many young English men and women to leave London and emigrate to the colonies.

FIGURE 1.2 *The Cheapside–Cornhill District of London, 1658*

1. Why was fire such a great danger in mid-seventeenth-century London? _____
   _____

2. How might life in such a city be different from life in a major city today?
   _____
   _____

3. Think about hygiene, food, and transportation. What smells would be different?
   Why? _____
   _____

   How was garbage and sewage removed? _____
   _____

   How was food prepared and sold? _____
   _____

   What smells would be absent that are present today? _____
   _____

   Was pollution worse or better? _____
   _____

   Did the city sound different then? _____
   _____

   **C** Seventeenth-century Europeans believed that the world was filled with spirits and demons. Many Christians, including educated officials and clergymen, feared that their neighbors consorted with the Devil and practiced witchcraft. Catholic and

Protestant magistrates tortured and executed suspected witches throughout Europe. Europeans brought their fears of witches to the American colonies.

The vast majority of the victims of the great witch scare were women, most often poor and very old, or very young. In 1652 a French court tried Suzanne Gaudry for witchcraft. At first she confessed, convinced by other peasants that a confession would save her. Later, realizing that the court intended to execute her regardless of what she said, she recanted her confession. The judges then ordered her tortured to find out whether she had told them the truth.

> This prisoner, before being strapped down, was admonished to maintain herself in her first confessions [to witchcraft] and to renounce [the devil]. She said she denies everything she has said [during her first forced confession] and that she has no lover [witches were assumed to have taken the devil as a lover]. Feeling herself being strapped down, says that she is not a witch, while struggling to cry.
>
> Asked why she fled outside [her village when the prosecutors came after her] says that God [forbids her to say she is a witch]. And upon being asked why she confessed to being one, said that she was forced to say it.
>
> Being a little stretched on the rack [a torture] screams ceaselessly that she is not a witch, invoking [God's name and the Virgin Mary]. Being more tightly stretched upon the torture rack, [and] urged to maintain her confessions, [she] said that it was true that she is a witch and that she would maintain what she [now] had said.[5]

1. What was Gaudry's suspected offense — what had she supposedly done?

   _____

   _____

2. In what ways was her treatment different from the treatment accorded a defendant today? _____

   _____

3. What made Gaudry change her testimony? _____

   _____

4. Does the passage suggest to you any reason why women were prosecuted for witchcraft ten times as often as men? _____

   _____

   _____

   _____

   _____

# Historical-Mindedness: The Discipline of History

As the study of history enables you to develop your sense of identity and recognize differences and similarities between the past and the present, you begin to confront some of your own prejudices about other peoples. Ironically, the more you study the past, the more prejudice and bias you encounter, for narrow-mindedness and hate were much in evidence in past times. You glimpsed this intolerance in the selections you read in exercise 3. Properly taught, history can reverse prejudice and help you understand the experiences of others.

True, you have certain values, and these dictate to a large extent how you see the past. You have in your mind a mental map of the outside world with visual and verbal signposts that enable you to process new information. If the study of history is to be possible at all, you must assume that you share with people from the past some similar ideas, attitudes, and views of the world, at least enough to be able to understand something of their experience. At the same time, the study of history sharpens your awareness of the differences between your mental map and those of people who lived in the past.

Historians call this imaginative intellectual endeavor "historical-mindedness," meaning that they try to see the past as those who lived in it saw it. Is this imaginative leap back in time really possible? We know that we can only see the past in our mind's eye. The "noble dream" of historical objectivity, to which past generations of "scientific historians" clung, held out the possibility of recapturing the past "as it actually was." Few historians still adhere to this position. However we may attempt to free ourselves of bias, however hard we may work to transcend the limitations of our mental map, we know we cannot reproduce the past in a test tube as a chemist in a laboratory can reproduce a chemical compound by following a formula. We can nevertheless strive to think critically and imaginatively about the past, and that enterprise is well worth the effort.

Your historical-mindedness will grow as you work through the exercises in *Reading and Writing American History*. At this stage of your study of historical methods, however, you are still dependent on what historians tell you. Your first step toward critical and imaginative thinking about the past requires you to begin to separate historical facts from historians' opinions. A historical fact is an educated conclusion about what happened in the past, reached through assembling pieces of historical evidence. Historical "facts" do not speak for themselves; they are statements historians make.

An opinion, by contrast, is a conviction, a persuasion, or a feeling that may or may not be based on fact but that rests on the writer's or speaker's own attitudes toward facts. It is a *judgment.* One historian's opinion about the past often differs from another historian's opinion precisely because opinion is an expression of the individual's state of mind. Historical-mindedness is an act of imaginative re-creation, and historical accounts will always feature both facts and opinions.

It is sometimes difficult to distinguish fact from opinion, but note the differences in the following examples. "It is raining today" is a factual statement about the weather. "It is a rotten day today" is an opinion about the weather. "The Puritans and the Indians mistrusted each other" is a historical fact. "The Indians should never have trusted the Puritans" is an opinion.

## EXERCISE 4: *Fact and Opinion*

Try your skill at separating fact from opinion. Read each passage, underline one fact, and circle one opinion in each. Be prepared to explain the reasons for your choices in class.

Note that the following selections are not original pieces of evidence (primary sources) but instead are taken from the work of historians. These are called secondary sources and are treated more fully in Chapter 3.

Ⓐ Nineteenth-century historian Francis Parkman wrote a series of books on the conflict between Native Americans and European emigrants in seventeenth- and eighteenth-century North America. He traveled the paths of the Iroquois and the Algonquin and read the accounts of English and French settlers, but he was no lover of Native American ways. A descendant of the founders of New England, he believed strongly that God and nature had ordained a British victory in the struggle against the Native Americans. Note, for example, his use of words like *savages* and *civilization*.

> In Indian social organization, a problem at once suggests itself. In these communities, comparatively populous, how could spirits so fierce, and in many respects, so un- governed, live together in peace, without law and without enforced authority? Yet there were towns where savages lived together in thousands, with a harmony which civilization might envy. This was in good measure due to peculiarities of the Indian character and habits. . . . That well-known self-control, which, originating in a form of pride, covered the savage nature of the man with a veil. . . . Though vain, arrogant, boastful, and vindictive, the Indian bore abuse and sarcasm with astonishing patience. Though greedy and grasping, he was lavish without stint, and would give away his all to . . . gain influence and applause, or ingratiate himself with his neighbors.[6]

**B** In the next selection, Professor Alden Vaughan of Columbia University, also a descendant of the founders of New England, comments on the same Native American peoples whom Parkman described. Vaughan focuses on the different ways in which Indians and Europeans waged war. The Native Americans fought small battles, little more than raids, for honor, to gain prisoners to replace lost population, or to persuade the vanquished to submit themselves to their victors. Europeans waged all-out war to control territory or scourge their religious enemies. There is a difference between Parkman's and Vaughan's mixture of facts and opin- ions that represents a century of growing sympathy for the Indians' rights and way of life between the time that Parkman and Vaughan wrote, but Vaughan is not an apologist for the Native Americans by any means.

> It may be that war among the New England tribes served more of a symbolic role than did European warfare [in Europe]. Various reasons for fighting [among the Indians] — petty grievances, revenge, defense of honor, and saving face — could perhaps be met by a show of courage without the wholesale slaughter that would only lead to prolonged and costly warfare. And since each tribe was small in mem- bership, it had strategic as well as humanitarian reasons to avoid heavy casualties; this undoubtedly encouraged the Indians to wage the cautious kind of battle that the [English in New England] found so ludicrous. While it is not true that the white man introduced the Indians to the art of war, it may well be that he taught the red man how to practice it more energetically.
>
> In contrast to the mildness of Indian warfare was the fury with which the red man destroyed many of their [male adult] captives. . . . Male captives were often tortured to death in ways more fiendish than any inquisitor [like the torturers of suspected witches] ever devised.[7]

**C** In this selection, Francis Jennings, until very recently director of the Native American Studies Program at the Newberry Library in Chicago, contributes his own general account of the relations between the English and the Native Americans. Jennings has little use for Vaughan's views and calls the confrontation between Native Americans and Europeans "the invasion of America." Does this give a clue to his opinion about who was at fault for the destruction of Native American ways of life? Was the arrival of the Europeans in fact an "invasion"? Underline a fact and circle an opinion.

> A basic rule was that any given Englishman at any given time formed his views [of Native Americans] in accordance with his purposes. Those who came for quick

plunder saw [Indian] plots and malignancy on every side; in a mirror image of their own intent, [these Englishmen's] savages were sinister and treacherous . . . much as the English saw Turks and Spaniards who were likewise fit objects of prey and likewise intransigent about accepting [the role the English assigned to them]. . . . When Indians were regarded as partners in a profitable trade, they appeared less threatening, and their vices were excused. When they resisted eviction from lands wanted by the colonizers, they acquired demonic dimensions. When they were wanted as soldiers for war against the French, the martial abilities of these [Indian] demons were appreciated rather than decried. In short, like the most modern of architects, the Englishman devised [an image of] the savage's form to fit [the Englishman's] function.[8]

Native American–European American relations are the subject of one of the saddest chapters in our history, sad because the encounter could have turned out much differently; because there were so many misconceptions on both sides; because no one really won — there were only victors and the vanquished; and because for so long historians failed to see through their own prejudices and their own need to give excuses for the many treacheries on both sides. Facing such gripping and argumentative points of view, how can you dissociate fact from opinion? Must you conclude that all historical arguments are just opinion, and therefore that one is just as true, or false, as another?

Historical mindedness, the goal of all history students, cannot provide you with absolute truths, but it will change you. It will teach you the difference between fact and opinion and help you to understand and appreciate the peoples of the past. To develop historical mindedness, you must begin with the same primary sources of history that historians use. The next chapter explores the varieties of primary sources, which are the building blocks of all historical knowledge.

## NOTES

1. Adapted from "He Whose Body is Divided in Twain," an Iroquois folk tale, reprinted in Frederick W. Turner III, ed., *The Portable North American Indian Reader* (New York: The Viking Press, 1973), 50–54.

2. William Bradford, *Of Plymouth Plantation, 1620–1647*, ed. Samuel Eliot Morison (New York: Modern Library, 1952), 3–4, 8, 10.

3. Lucien Febvre, "History and Psychology" in Febvre, *A New Kind of History and Other Essays*, ed. Peter Burke, trans. K. Folca (New York: Harper & Row, 1973), 7–8.

4. Brother Luis Brandaon to Father Sandoval, March 12, 1610, in Elizabeth Donnan, ed., *Documents Illustrative of the History of the Slave Trade to America* (Washington D.C.: Carnegie Institute, 1930), 1:123–124.

5. Alan C. Kors and Edward Peters, eds., *Witchcraft in Europe, 1100–1700: A Documentary History* (Philadelphia: University of Pennsylvania Press, 1972), 274–275.

6. Francis Parkman, *The Jesuits in North America* [1867] in Samuel Eliot Morison, ed., *The Parkman Reader* (Boston: Little, Brown and Co., 1955), 41.

7. Alden T. Vaughan, *New England Frontier, Puritans and Indians, 1620–1675* (rev. ed. New York: W. W. Norton, 1979), 40.

8. Francis Jennings, *The Invasion of America: Indians, Colonization, and the Cant of Conquest* (Chapel Hill, N.C.: University of North Carolina Press, 1975), 59.

# 2 EVIDENCE OF THE PAST: PRIMARY SOURCES

## *The Colonial Period*

There is an old Japanese tale about a warrior and his wife who are attacked in the woods by a bandit. No one questions the end result: the husband had been killed, the wife abused, and the bandit captured, but when the magistrates try to find out what happened, they get conflicting stories. The bandit boasts of his bravery; the wife calls him and her husband cowards and clowns; and the ghost of the husband protests that his conduct was honorable. Finally, a woodsman appears who had seen the whole affair from a hiding place in the bushes. He contradicts all the other stories and the magistrates believe him. Unbeknownst to the magistrates, he too had a reason to lie: he had found and kept the warrior's beautiful knife. Everyone had a different perspective on what happened and, perhaps, a reason to lie as strong as any reason to tell the truth.

The historian, like the magistrates in the Japanese story, begins with evidence. The evidence may be oral or written. Eyewitnesses may be lying or trying to tell the truth. Even a witness who wants to see everything and tell all is handicapped by the limitations of being human. A favorite trick of professors who teach criminal law is to "stage" a crime in class and then have all the students write down what they saw. Invariably, no two accounts are exactly alike.

How is the historian to piece together a reasonable account of past events based on such fallible evidence? Daunted by the prospect, some cynical observers conclude that history is not worth studying, and then cite historical examples to prove the truth of their claim! Other, more extreme, critics of history have even argued that there is no past — only the present. We need only turn to the bedrock of historical evidence — the primary source — to prove that it is possible to know something about the past.

## Survivals from the Past

The pieces of original evidence that the historian finds and weighs to build facts are called the primary sources of history. A primary source is material — a document or other evidence — that was created during the period or the event that the

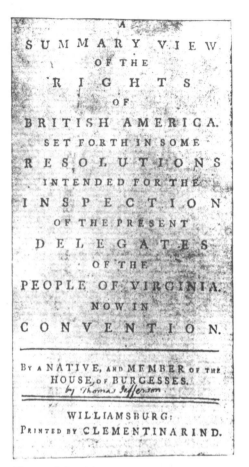

**FIGURE 2.1** *Title Page from Thomas Jefferson's Pamphlet "Summary View"*

historian is studying. As long as the piece of evidence was produced during the time under investigation, it is a primary source.

Primary sources come in many shapes and sizes. Some may be written documents — for example, newspapers, legislative records, or a court's opinions. Last wills and testaments penned in spidery-thin and shaky handwriting are just as much primary sources as leather- and gold-bound first editions of famous books. A primary source can be private — for example, a diary or a letter from a parent to a child — or public, such as an act of Congress or a presidential address. Finally, a primary source can be a physical artifact, such as a piece of furniture, a building, or a painting.

Some primary sources were meant to be private but became public, and their publication changed the course of events. One such source was a secret letter from the royal governor of the colony of Massachusetts, Thomas Hutchinson, to his friends in London, warning them that the Sons of Liberty in Boston were planning riots to oppose English rule. Nothing came of Hutchinson's warning — until Benjamin Franklin came upon the private letter and arranged to publish it in a Boston newspaper. When people in Massachusetts read the letter, they were outraged. Protests erupted and Hutchinson's warnings came true.

Sometimes the public, official world and the private, domestic world come together in primary sources. The documents shown in Figures 2.1 and 2.2 — a title page of one of the most famous pamphlets urging American colonists to resist

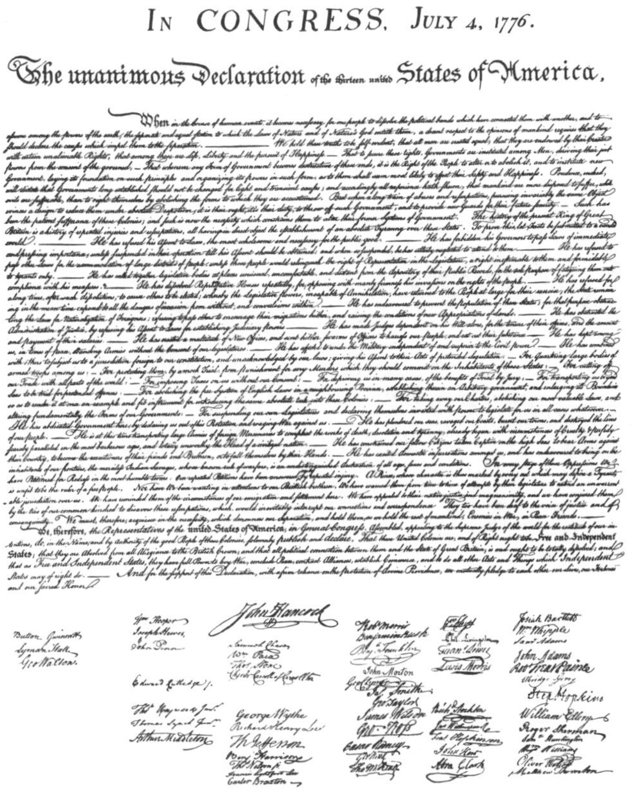

IN CONGRESS, JULY 4, 1776.

The unanimous Declaration of the thirteen united States of America.

FIGURE 2.2 *Engrossed (final handwritten) copy of the Declaration of Independence*

Parliament on the eve of the Revolution, and the Declaration of Independence itself — were both private and public. Neither was the work of a government, yet both led to the creation of the most powerful state on the face of the earth. Notice that the pamphlet was printed and the Declaration was handwritten. Both are primary sources for our study of the revolutionary movement.

Primary sources for American history can be understood and enjoyed for themselves. You can get a good deal of pleasure and instruction from reading the essays of Franklin, for example, or wandering the grounds of the great Virginia plantations of the eighteenth century. As students of history, you must do much more with primary sources; you must use them to understand the people who created them. Primary sources are original evidence, and evidence must be examined critically. You cannot just believe the woodcutter's tale.

The first section of this chapter will introduce you to two types of primary sources: textual and visual. The chapter will then discuss common problems in verifying and interpreting primary sources.

The tangible, physical remains of primary sources for the study of early American history are all around you. The charter that King James of England granted to the Virginia Company of Plymouth — the legal basis for the Pilgrim and Puritan settlements in the New World — is preserved with loving care in the Massachusetts statehouse. The weathered clapboard family house of Rebecca Nurse, one of the victims of the Salem witchcraft trials of 1692, still stands just outside the modern town of Danvers, Massachusetts. The problem is that these primary sources no longer really fit in with their surroundings. The old charter is protected from thieves by a glass display case unlike any that the Puritans possessed, and at the Essex County (Massachusetts) Historical Society you can purchase T-shirts depicting the Nurse family homestead. Given this mixture of old and new, how do you pick out a primary source from its modern surroundings?

## EXERCISE 1: *Identifying Primary Sources*

Following are two sets of documents, each set containing a primary source and a later historian's account of a contemporaneous event. As you decide which is which, think about the definition of primary sources. What clues can you gain from the passage to help you decide?

**A** Roger Williams was a Puritan minister whose spiritual strength and magnetic personality won him a great following when he came to Massachusetts in 1631. His opinions on religious conformity, particularly his unwillingness to let the colony's government in Boston tell him and his parishioners what to believe and how to worship, threatened political order in the colony and induced Governor John Winthrop of Massachusetts to warn Williams against further protests. Williams continued to battle for the rights of conscience, forgave Winthrop, fled Massachusetts, and set about making Providence Plantation (the Rhode Island colony) a haven for victims of religious persecution. Although Williams and Winthrop were antagonists throughout this episode, the two men genuinely admired and liked each other, and each hoped that the other could be persuaded of the error of his ways.

1. To Winthrop this [religious] liberalism [of Williams's] was . . . ridiculous . . . Williams's views on civil government had degraded the holy purpose of the state; now [Williams] degraded the still holier purpose of the church, welcoming the mixed multitude [to services] . . . To Winthrop and to other New England Puritans of the 1630s such was the counsel not of wisdom but of despair and defeat, the very thing to be expected from a man like Williams, who leaped always from one extreme to another.[1]

2. To Every courteous reader: While I plead the cause of truth and innocencie against the bloody doctrine of persecution for cause of conscience, I judge it not unfit to give alarme to my selfe, and all men to prepare to be persecuted or hunted for cause of conscience . . . Who can now but expect that after so many scores of years preaching and professing of more truth, and amongst so many great contentions amongst the very best of Protestants, a fierie furnace should be heat[ed], and who sees not now the fires kindling?[2]

Which of these two passages is the primary source? _____ Why? _____

_____

**B** Williams and Winthrop agreed on one fact — there was a Devil and he had the power to intrude into people's affairs. He could cause disease and disruption in a household and in an entire colony. He could possess people, and only a true faith and a willing spirit could hold him at bay. Throughout the seventeenth century, the New England colonies of Massachusetts and Connecticut experienced periodic outbreaks of suspected witchcraft, and everyone believed the Devil was behind the troubles.

1. In their front-line struggle against the Devil and his legions, New Englanders labored under severe handicaps. Theirs was a supremely difficult task because the enemy was so devious, so shrewd, so resourceful in his methods of attack. His strategy was endlessly varied and surprising; he missed no opportunity for destructive intervention in human affairs. He possessed, moreover, the great advantage of being *invisible* to those whom he strove to subdue. The term most frequently applied to him, "Prince of Darkness," served to characterize both his ends and his means.[3]

2. Thursday night, being the 27th day of November [1679], we heard a great noise without against the house; whereupon myself and wife looked out and saw nobody . . . but we had stones and sticks thrown at us [so] that we were forced to retire into the house . . . [four days later] in the afternoon pots hanging over the fire did dash so vehemently one against the other [that] we set down one that they might not dash to pieces. I saw the andiron leap into the pot and dance and leap out, and again leap in and dance and leap out again . . . [We saw] a tub . . . fly off of itself, and the tub turn over and nobody near it.[4]

Which passage is the primary source? _____ Why? _____

# The Variety of Primary Sources

The variety of primary sources provides much of the joy of studying history. There is something for everyone's taste. Primary sources describe war and peace, leisure and work, the intimacy of family life, and the bustle of strange, crowded meeting places. In short, primary sources are as varied as the people who created them. The more you know about the time and the people from which the primary sources come, the better you can understand the sources, but written sources often have a charm or compelling power that seems to span time itself.

### EXERCISE 2: *When History Speaks to Us*

The following three passages are primary sources about the lives of ordinary people in the eighteenth-century English North American colonies. These readings appeal to us because we share the joy, wonder, and humor of the author. Read each passage carefully. What do the passages tell you about the activities and attitudes of their authors? Beneath each passage, write two observations of your own about these authors' worlds based on information you have taken from the passages.

**A** The author of the first passage was an eleven-year-old girl from a very well-to-do New England family. Her name was Anna Green Winslow, and when her father, mother, and brother left her in the care of a Boston aunt to finish her schooling, Anna began a diary. In it, she recorded the hopes and fears of a girl about to enter a world that subordinated women to men. Anna died of tuberculosis in 1779, at the age of nineteen.

Feb. 9th, 1772. . . . My honored Mamma will be so good as to excuse my using the pen of my old friend just here, because I am disabled by a [sore] on my fourth finger and something like one on my middle finger, from using my own pen; but altho my right hand is in bondage, my left is free; and my aunt says, it will be a nice opportunity if I do but improve [on] it, to perfect myself in learning to spin flax. . . . My fingers are not the only part of me that has suffered with sores within this fortnight, for I have had a great ugly boil upon my right hip and about a dozen small ones . . . I am at present swathed hip and thigh, as Samson smote the Philistines, but my soreness is near over . . . I have to read my Bible to my aunt this morning (as is the daily custom) and sometimes I read other books to her. So you may perceive, I have the use of my tongue and I tell her it is a good thing to have the use of my tongue.[5]

Observation 1: _____

Observation 2: _____

**B** The second passage comes from the hand of Philip Vickers Fithian, a New Jersey college student who secured a place as a tutor to the children of one of Virginia's richest planters, Landon Carter. Fithian was bemused, delighted, appalled, and kept on his toes not only by his young students, but by the master of the house as well.

Rose by seven, sent for [the] barber and was drest for breakfast — we went to breakfast at ten — I confess I have been seldom more dashed than when I entered the dining-room, for I must of necessity be interrogated [by Carter] . . . about my [health] . . . After breakfast we all retired into the dancing-room, and after the [students] had their lesson . . . there were several minuets danced with great ease and propriety; after which the whole company joined in country-dances, and it was indeed beautiful to . . . see such a number of young persons, set off by dress to the best advantage, moving easily, to the sound of well performed music, and with perfect regularity, tho' apparently in the utmost disorder.[6]

Observation 1: _____

Observation 2: _____

**C** The third primary source is an old Puritan minister's recollection of his school days. John Barnard was expected, like every New England Puritan boy, to study hard, behave well, and go to church. In the following episode he recounts how he found a way to bend the rules to his advantage.

Though my [school-]master advanced me . . . yet I was a very naughty boy, much given to play, insomuch that he at length openly declared, ". . . I know you can do well enough if you will; but you are so full of play that you hinder your classmates from getting their lessons [done]; and therefore, if any of them cannot perform their duty, I shall correct you for it." One unlucky day one of my classmates did not look into his book and therefore could not say his lesson, though I called upon him once and again to mind his book; upon which our master beat me. . . . The boy was pleased with my being corrected, and persisted in his neglect, for which I was still corrected, and that for several days. I thought, in justice, I ought to correct the boy, and compel him to a better temper; and therefore, after school was done, I went up to him, and told him I had been beaten several times for his neglect, and since master would not correct him I would . . . and then drubbed him heartily.[7]

Observation 1: _____

Observation 2: _____

# Seeing the Past

To some extent, written primary sources speak for themselves. You might assume that visual primary sources would be even easier to understand than letters and diaries, but maps, pictures, and material remains (buildings, home and workplace furnishings, tools, and other "artifacts") are actually more difficult to use as primary sources than are documents. Visual sources can be rich repositories of past customs and attitudes, but you must look hard to see deeply into them.

The creators of visual primary sources were expressing their own views, communicating a message to persuade or entertain an audience or capture an idea. Pictures of old buildings, roads, or fields do not reveal untouched nature but an artificial human ordering of objects in space. Settlers chose sites for houses not only with wood, water, and food supply in mind, but also to impose a human plan on the natural world. The first European villages in the New World were invariably surrounded by wooden walls or earthen embankments — barriers to keep unwanted visitors out. Later, wealthy colonists built big houses in plain sight of their poorer neighbors (unlike modern mansions deliberately constructed in secluded places) for a reason. John Hancock, the richest man in colonial Massachusetts, and George Washington, the richest man in colonial Virginia, both erected their houses on hills, not just to enjoy the view, but to demonstrate their status and authority to everyone else in their communities.

## EXERCISE 3: *Visualizing Life in and Around the Big House*

The two illustrations in this exercise depict great plantation houses in tidewater (coastal) Virginia. Not many planters could afford to build on such a scale, but all aspired to live in grand style. The living spaces and workplaces of many of the wealthy planters of the colonial South were both functional and symbolic. The great planters were a small minority of the free population of the southern tidewater, but they were the leaders of that society. They built near the water in order to ship their tobacco crops directly to English and Scottish ports. The size and geometric regularity of their homes were intended to give visual proof of their right to rule. The visual impact of their houses reinforced the planters' status in society.

The large plantation was a village in itself, with smokehouses, storerooms, blacksmith's and carpenter's shops, and rows of wooden cabins for slaves. Day laborers and tenants did not live on the grounds of the great house but had their own cabins on the plantation. Authority on the plantation descended from the big house to all corners of the planter's domain. The common folk mingled with the gentry in market towns and in churches, taverns, and courthouses, but the focal point of society was the great house.

Figure 2.3 is a sample of "folk art," a homemade painting dating from the end of the eighteenth century. Figure 2.4 is a modern photograph of a restored plantation house, Westover. Both concern the same object but convey the importance of the big house in different ways. Examine these visual primary sources and answer the questions following each.

At the top of the painting is the great house, and along the sides of the hill are the outbuildings, including slave quarters. What does this arrangement seem to say about the relationship between the master and the servants and slaves?

**FIGURE 2.3** *"The Plantation" (1825)*

**FIGURE 2.4** *Westover, Home of the William Byrd Family*

In the painting, the entire hill seems to rest on water — at its bottom is a river wide and deep enough to support a three-masted sailing ship. Next to the ship is a tobacco warehouse. What does the arrangement of these objects suggest about the source of the planter's wealth?

_____

_____

The William Byrd family house is a three-story, red-brick mansion, built on the same ground on which Byrd's father constructed a frame house, the falls of the James River. The younger Byrd pursued political power and wealth avidly, and though he never became the English nobleman he dreamed of being, he did achieve prominence in Virginia politics.

1. How did his new residence symbolize his importance? _____

_____

2. Imagine that you are approaching the front door. What impressions would you

   have? _____

_____

# Evaluating Primary Sources

The textual and visual primary sources you encountered in the previous pages seem authentic, but there is always the possibility that they are not genuine. There are famous forgeries that still haunt historians. Not so long ago one of the most respected of English historians tried to authenticate Adolf Hitler's "Diaries." These diaries supposedly proved that Hitler never intended to commit genocide. A few weeks later, when the forger was revealed, this historian issued a qualified apology.

Forgers have faked letters from Jefferson, Lincoln, and Washington. Sets of documents have been forged as well, as in the notorious case of the *Horn Papers*. The three volumes of *Horn Papers*, describing explorations in western Pennsylvania from 1765 to 1795, were not what they appeared to be. In 1945, a year after their publication, Julian P. Boyd, a historian, charged that they were composed of fictitious letters, journals, and maps. He was correct. The forger, never identified, had fooled everyone else, but not Boyd. Later, scholars concluded that "it is apparent that the creator of the diaries and the maps carefully worked over the modern geological survey maps and may even have traced portions of them."[8]

The first clues to a source's authenticity are physical characteristics. Is the document or artifact old enough to be dated from the period it supposedly came from? Was it found in an appropriate place? Does it use the language of the times, or was it the product of tools used in that period? Is the handwriting genuine? A good way to authenticate a primary source is to compare it with similar sources that have already been authenticated, although the most interesting forgeries are those that materially add to or contradict existing sources. Another conventional way to test the legitimacy of a primary source is to find references to it in other, well-established sources. The new source then fills a gap in the chain of evidence. Keep in mind, though, that such gaps can be invitations to forgers.

## *Point of View*

The vast majority of surviving primary sources are genuine, but every primary source reveals its own point of view. Whether or not the author of a document sought to gain some advantage or mislead someone else, like the woodcutter in the story at the beginning of this chapter, a particular perspective and position in life colors everyone's observations and expressions. Sometimes a primary source is obviously colored by the prejudices of its author; at other times the source's originator may have been badly positioned to see and describe an event.

Although every primary source has a point of view, reading it critically enables you to recognize and avoid the most common pitfalls. The basic principles of "source criticism" can be reduced to the following seven questions you can ask about every primary source you encounter:

1. Was the person who created the source well positioned to know what was happening? Was he or she well acquainted with the people and places described? Was the author one of the group at the center of the event or a mere observer? Did he or she have access to other documents and other observers?

2. Have other documents or letters written by that person proved to be accurate? Some famous men and women have proved to be notorious liars, and the number of primary materials that include gossip or outright fantasy is immense.

3. Did the author have a personal interest in what he or she was describing that would color the account (or lead to a lie)? Even if the author intended to be objective, such interests would influence what the author thought he or she heard and saw and would undermine the reliability of even a firsthand account.

4. What sort of language does the author of a written account employ? Is it hysterical or calm, angry or sympathetic? If the source is an example of a particular literary genre, such as a novel or a poem, the author has probably rearranged facts — people and settings — for literary effect. (Even a work of fiction can be a primary source of attitudes or literary conventions.) If the work is a picture, how much has the artist's style altered reality? Have dramatic conventions replaced facts?

5. Was the source created immediately, within a short span of time, or many years after the event it describes? (Many primary accounts are recollections by participants or observers in their old age, and psychological studies have shown that we often lose 70 percent of our memory of a particular event within the first 24 hours after seeing or hearing it.)

6. To whom is the account or visual depiction addressed? What was the intended or expected audience? Many documents are written to persuade or reassure a particular audience. For example, although his quarrel was with ministers in neighboring Massachusetts, Roger Williams sent many of his sermons and letters to England to be published so that influential Puritans there might understand why he defended freedom of worship.

7. Finally, what impact did the words or pictures have on their actual audience? Historians have become very sensitive to the changing meaning of common words. Books and pamphlets written in English more than 300 years ago do not always use words in the same way that we use them today. For example, to the seventeenth-century American colonists the word *constitution* was the body of English and American law; today it means a written foundation of government. We retain the earlier meaning when we talk about a person having "a sound constitution."

## EXERCISE 4: *Point of View and Reliability*

This exercise asks you to assess the reliability of one of the most famous primary sources depicting the struggle between the British and the French for control of

**FIGURE 2.5** *Benjamin West,* **The Death of General Wolfe** *(1770)*

North America. Figure 2.5 shows Benjamin West's deeply moving and justly famous painting *The Death of General Wolfe* (1770), painted eleven years after Wolfe died leading his troops against the French in Canada. Wolfe, dying in the center foreground, is surrounded by his generals and illuminated by a streak of sunlight piercing an otherwise grey and forbidding sky. Beyond him the battle rages. In the foreground a Native American contemplates the scene.

Comment on the impression the picture makes.

1. What emotion does it evoke in you? _____

_____

2. What impression do you gain of Wolfe? _____

_____

Of his officers' feeling for him? _____

_____

Benjamin West was not present when the battle he depicted took place, but he might have gathered the details of Wolfe's death from those who were at the scene. Did he? The crowds that gathered to view the painting at the Royal Academy exhibition room in England on April 29, 1771, thought West's work brilliant. Indeed, West, a Pennsylvanian who had come to England to learn to paint and who had gained the support of King George III, had used every artistic convention he could to heighten the drama of Wolfe's dying moments. The grouping of the central figures draws every viewer's eye to Wolfe's final agony. The use of light and shadow, even the opportune opening of the heavens to shine a ray of sun on Wolfe's face, adds to the total effect.

West's Wolfe was a hero, dying a hero's death, and that assuaged the gnawing doubts that many British leaders had about the appalling expense of the French and Indian war. Britain still staggered under the debt and looked to the American colonists to pay off part of it. What is more, until Wolfe's near miraculous victory, symbolized in the painting by the heavenly light shining on the dying general, British armies in the American wilderness had not fought well. In effect, West's painting offered a history of the war that justified Britain's sacrifices to drive the French from North America.

But was West's history reliable? Certain facts regarding the war are indisputable. On the plains of Abraham above the French colonial citadel of Quebec a battle was fought that determined the fate of both the French and the English empires in North America. The French and Indian war had already dragged on for four years, with early French successes giving way to a bloody stalemate, when, in 1758, the English thrust at the French colony of Canada, sealing it off from the French homeland. Rugged French-Canadian farmers, woodsmen, and their Indian allies, along with a handful of regular French troops, continued to defend Montreal and Quebec, however.

The next year, after a spring and summer of fruitless attempts to lure French General Montcalm out of the fortress of Quebec, English commander James Wolfe boldly sailed his expeditionary force down the St. Lawrence River past the city. During the night his rangers and Highlander (Scottish) troops scaled a two-hundred foot cliff to attack the city from above. The French charged out of their fortifications at dawn on September 13, 1759, but the British held their ground and were victorious. Wolfe, along with his great adversary Montcalm, died in the fighting.

From first-hand accounts, historian Simon Schama has pieced together a composite of the actual circumstances of Wolfe's death, as voiced by a soldier:

> Then up comes the captain and tells me to take a message to the general [Wolfe] to say our line had held and the enemy was put to flight. And I had rather it had been another man; I was tired at all we had done last night and this morning. But I obeyed and ran over the field stepping through blood and faces upturned in death and a few horses, poor beasts their bellies all spilld open. . . . when suddenly I saw him, lying on a mound beside a sorry little bush attended by just two men, one leaning over and supporting Wolfe with his arm. . . . I approached Wolfe and saw his face had gone stiff and greenish and his red hair glistened with sun and sweat. Blood had matted his belly where another ball had struck him. . . . seeing he would not live I told him our news and in a groaning gurgling sort of way I could hear him praise God for it.[9]

In life Wolfe had been unsuccessful in most of what he did. Though still in his thirties when he died, he had never won a great battle. Gawky (he resembled the Washington Irving character Ichabod Crane), melancholic, and plagued by stomach ailments, he had a premonition that he would never return from Canada to his beloved England. When the news of the battle reached Britain and her colonies, Wolfe in death became what he never was in life — a hero.

Look again at Figure 2.5. Notice how it differs from the account that Schama presents. Did West take liberties with the evidence available to him? Your answers to the following study questions will help you gauge the reliability of West's famous painting.

1. Was West well situated to know what happened to Wolfe? Was West close to the events he depicted? _____

_____

2. Did West have any personal interest in altering what he was told about the general's death? _____

_____

3. Is West's portrayal of Wolfe's death overly dramatic? _____

_____

4. Did West paint the picture soon after the events occurred? _____

_____

5. For what audience did West paint? Did West intend his work to have any particular impact on that audience? _____

_____

6. Did West use any stylistic or other artistic conventions to heighten the impact of the painting? _____

_____

7. How reliable do you find West's depiction of the death of Wolfe? _____

_____

## Point in Time

The seven rules of source criticism and exercise 4 raise the issue of the context of primary sources. A historically minded reader or viewer of a primary source tries to imagine how it appeared in its original surroundings. This historical setting is the context of the source. For example, you gain a deeper understanding of the Salem witch trials by standing in the restored houses and churches of Danvers, Massachusetts. There, amid the dark-timbered, low-ceiling homes of the Puritans, you can see how closely people lived to one another and how resentments and rivalries could turn into accusations of witchcraft.

The most obvious context of a primary source is the point in time at which the author of the source created it. The actual period of time in which that person lived, as you learned in Chapter 1, influenced what he or she had to say about any subject. Examples of such time spans are centuries, decades, and years. Historians take these actual spans of time and turn them into historical periods. Historical periods provide a way to divide time into segments, in order to group distinct events and ideas together and separate them from other, different groups of events and ideas. For example, historians use centuries as a shorthand way to distinguish periods of human conduct and ideas. The fixed period of time — the century — becomes a symbol of critical changes or innovations in human thought. Thus historians speak of "seventeenth-century rationality," which refers to the movement by some philosophers, scientists, and teachers of the period to replace religious faith with scientific experiment as the highest form of mental activity.

Historians also separate centuries into decades and try to characterize each decade with a central theme. The 1930s becomes the Great Depression decade, the 1960s the decade of protest movements, and the 1980s the "me first" decade. Historians may turn the actual span of time in office of kings or presidents into a historical period, presuming that the political leader created or captured the mood of the era. For example, historians use the phrase "Jacksonian era" to denote the period when Andrew Jackson dominated American politics. The "Reagan era" is synonymous with the period 1980–1988. Historians also divide time into "ages" and "eras" characterized by important events and movements. Examples of such periodization are "the space age" and "the Cold War era."

To begin re-creating the context of a primary source, you must "date" it, but as you have learned, there are many ways to periodize any source. Although centuries, decades, and years may seem to be objective or neutral names for time spans, the symbolic impact of phrases like "the Age of Discovery" goes beyond mere chronology to imply a substantive unity to a period of time. "The Age of Discovery" refers to the era during which European explorers reached the coasts of the Americas, Africa, and Asia. For Europeans, the news that the world could be circumnavigated was a great discovery, but for modern historians to say that "Columbus discovered America" is to ignore the 10 million Native Americans who lived and flourished in what is now North and South America *before* Columbus pridefully claimed any of their lands for the king of Spain.

By varying the historical period into which you place any primary source, you vary the group of events, lives, and ideas that surround the source — in effect you alter its context. In so doing, you can change the shades of meaning the primary source exhibits. For example, if you place the Declaration of Independence in the "Age of Revolution," you link it to the French Revolution, which occurred in 1789. The Declaration thus becomes the model for the radical French Declaration of Rights. If, instead, you decide that the Declaration was the closing chapter of "the Colonial era," you root it in 200 years of English colonial history and cut it off from later European radicalism.

### EXERCISE 5: *Periodization*

Despite the dangers of too grand or too narrow periodization, historians must place primary sources in some chronological context, some period. For this exercise, look through the first two chapters of your textbook and find three examples of periodization. In the space provided, explain what the author means by the terms he or she uses.

1. _____

   _____

2. _____

   _____

3. _____

   _____

# Imagining Absent Sources

For every primary source that survives the ravages of time, an incalculable number are lost. War, fire, rain, insects, and rodents are great ravagers of original evidence. Just as you throw out old newspapers and magazines when you clean your room, so people in the past threw out documents that would fascinate modern historians and students. In the end, only a tiny portion of all that people have used and created survives.

Think about how certain types of primary sources seem to survive, while others vanish. Official documents tend to survive because governments make an effort to preserve such items as tax lists, laws and court decisions, and administrative memoranda. These public records are often kept in safe places and watched by specially appointed guardians, while private documents — letters from one family member to another, for example — often survive only by chance.

There are even deeper patterns of human relationships that explain the existence — and absence — of certain kinds of primary sources. Wealth, education, and power directly influence the likelihood that a primary source will survive. Poor people in early history were almost always illiterate. They could not keep diaries, write letters, or prepare inventories of their few possessions. Women, often denied educational opportunities, also left relatively little evidence of their thoughts and feelings. Racial minorities in early America — Native Americans, African Americans, and Asian Americans — developed rich and varied oral cultures, but their words do not survive as do many official documents or the correspondence of the wealthy and powerful. Historians interested in the everyday lives of the poor, women, and racial minorities must dig into church registers, tax rolls, and militia lists — places where the many did leave their mark.

Absent sources are also hidden sources — hidden by layers of later human activity and by even thicker layers of subsequent local lore. For example, the "Five Points" area of lower Manhattan was a lively place in the early nineteenth century — thickly populated, full of life, noisy, and dangerous. For much of the twentieth century, however, Five Points was literally covered over by courthouses and office buildings. The neighborhood seemed almost eerie in its silence when evening came. In the 1980s, renovators tore down a block of the twentieth-century buildings and came upon the remains of the early nineteenth-century settlement. The foundations of old houses and bits of glassware, pottery, furniture, and ironwork revealed a world long thought lost — a world in which poor people lived, worked, and died.

When lost sources are ignored in the stories that local residents tell, it is even harder for the historian to reconstruct the past. In 1985, Timothy H. Breen, a leading colonial historian, was invited to serve as a resident researcher at the East Hampton (New York) Historical Society. East Hampton is a rapidly changing township on the southeastern end of Long Island. Founded in the 1650s as a fishing and farming village by Puritans from New England, it has become a fashionable resort for the rich and famous. Defenders of its old ways wanted Professor Breen to recover a purer, simpler past, but instead he found many layers of self-deception that obscured, rather than revealed, the history of the first town. East Hampton's modern residents had come to believe that the town had been a backwater — a stable, close-knit, farming community of English men and women. Breen found that they were wrong. The community in fact had been multiracial — Native Americans and African Americans had lived among the New England settlers — but local historians had bit by bit forgotten about the minorities. In addition, colonial East Hampton was not a backwater but part of a commercial network stretching across the Atlantic Ocean. By the end of the colonial era, its fishermen had literally decimated the herds of right whales that migrated along its shores to supply Europe with candle wax and other commodities. Breen concluded that his sources were not only buried in the sands and woods but concealed under layers of local tradition:

> In early East Hampton the process [of people telling stories about themselves] probably involved a kind of informal oral history. People shared remembered traditions [of the founders of the village]. . . . At some point local historians began to put the stories into written form, and, as they did so, they often organized the facts in new ways. . . . Over time interpretations . . . were amalgamated into a popular understanding of the [harmonious], communal past, and it eventually became impossible to distinguish the actual past from stories that local historians had written about the past. And slowly, almost imperceptibly, the accretion of interpretation gave birth to mythology.[10]

The relative paucity of sources about the lives of the great majority of people in the past is a serious problem for any student of history. Wealthy planters and merchants kept diaries and ledger books, corresponded with each other, and served in government posts. They wrote laws and edited newspapers. The vast majority of colonists, however, were hard-working farmers, housewives, day laborers, crafts-people, servants, slaves, and children. They did not leave diaries or letters, but they built furniture, used cooking utensils, rocked their children in cradles, and purchased pitchers and bowls. When such objects survive, we call them artifacts, and they are evidence of the vernacular (common) material culture of a people.

Many of these artifacts from eighteenth-century life have survived. The most elegant of them are highly valued as antiques, although almost every family possessed some tools, furniture, and pots and pans. We can even date when a family lived in a house by the kind of cups and plates they used and the jugs and jars in which they stored food. For example, until the early 1700s, most Americans ate with wooden utensils from small wooden trays called "trenchers." By the 1720s, however, even the poorest families could afford ceramic plates.

## EXERCISE 6: *Interpreting Artifacts*

Look at the pictures of eighteenth-century artifacts reproduced in Figure 2.6. In the space below each picture, describe what you see in your own words. How would your life be different if your world were filled with these material things? Imagine yourself using them — the joy of studying history is exercising your imagination.

Now that you have confronted some of the problems that primary sources raise, consider again the relationship between these sources — the historian's evidence — and the historical fact. Even the most interesting primary sources do not really tell their own story. They must be molded and shaped to build facts. Then the facts must be arrayed into arguments that persuade or enlighten readers. A simple mental experiment confirms that primary sources are only the raw materials of history. Imagine that you had the supernatural power to bring every primary source back from its time. You would discover that for every source that led to one conclusion, you could find another contradicting it. The only way you could make sense of all your evidence would be to select among the primary sources, arrange your selections in some order, and decide which pieces of evidence to emphasize. This process is what historians engage in when they produce secondary sources, the subject of the next chapter.

## NOTES

1. Edmund S. Morgan, *The Puritan Dilemma: The Story of John Winthrop* (Boston: Little, Brown, 1958), 132.
2. Roger Williams, *The Bloudy Tenent of Persecution* [1643], reprinted in Perry Miller and Thomas H. Johnson, eds., *The Puritans* (New York: Harper & Row, 1963), 1:216.
3. John P. Demos, *Entertaining Satan: Witchcraft and the Culture of Early New England* (New York: Oxford University Press, 1982), 97.
4. Ibid., 132–133.
5. *Diary of Anna Green Winslow: A Boston School Girl of 1771*, ed. Alice Morse Earle (Boston: Houghton Mifflin, 1985), 20–21.

**FIGURE 2.6** *Eighteenth-century Spinning Wheel, Warming Pan, and Toasting Iron*

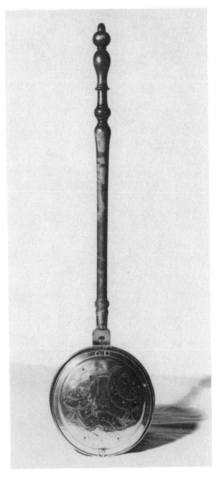

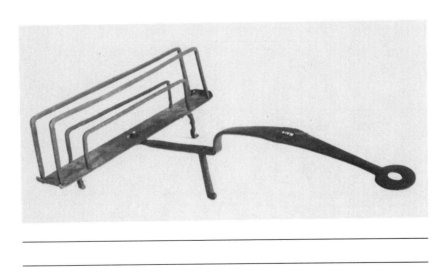

6. Philip Vickers Fithian, *Journal and Letters of Philip Vickers Fithian* [1773–1774], ed. H. D. Farrish (Charlottesville: University Press of Virginia, 1957), 33.

7. "Autobiography of the Rev. John Barnard," *Collections of the Massachusetts Historical Society,* 3rd ser. 5 (1836), 178–219.

8. Douglass Adair and Arthur Pierce Middleton, "The Mystery of the Horn Papers," in *William and Mary Quarterly,* 3rd ser. 4 (1947), 445.

9. Simon Schama, *Dead Certainties* (New York: Knopf, 1991), 68–69.

10. Timothy H. Breen, *Imagining the Past: East Hampton Histories* (Reading, Mass.: Addison-Wesley, 1989), 39.

# 3 THE HISTORIAN'S WORK: SECONDARY SOURCES

## Causes and Consequences of the American Revolution

Thomas Jefferson played a leading role in the American and French revolutions — two upheavals that gave birth to the modern world — ran a large business, designed the campus for the University of Virginia, supervised a thoroughgoing revision of the laws of his state, kept extensive astronomical and botanical notebooks, reared two daughters after his wife died, served as president of the United States of America, and still found time to be a historian. Understandably, Jefferson insisted that only those who had taken part in important events should write history. His rule would bar most modern historians from practicing their craft. Fortunately for today's historians, Jefferson's premise — that only those close to power can know how power is used — is out of date. In our own day, when the world is no farther from us than our televisions, radios, and newspapers, all of us have the chance to eavesdrop on the secrets of the mighty and sympathize with the sufferings of the many.

The books, articles, and lectures that historians write and deliver are the secondary sources of history. To the original evidence, the primary sources, the historian brings specialized training, craftsmanship, and intellect. The writing of secondary sources is simultaneously painstaking and exciting, arduous and engrossing. There are moments when every historian shares Simon Schama's near despair that "we are doomed to be forever hailing someone who has just gone around the corner and out of earshot."[1] Yet there are other moments that reward our labor, when we are seized by what Timothy Breen recently termed "a nervous inspiration" and grasp, in a blinding flash of light, the connection between past and present.[2]

## The Variety of Secondary Sources

Jefferson had faith that the study of history was a vital part of every political leader's education. For him, history taught imperishable truths about human motivation and the fate of nations. After he left the office of president of the United States in 1809, he dedicated himself to the study of history and urged young people to do likewise, arguing that history was the great storehouse of human experience.

Because he believed that people could and should learn from history, Jefferson admonished historians to do more than simply tell a story. They must also explain the meaning of that story. Jefferson's rule is still binding: the historian is duty-bound to explore the causes and consequences of human action.

## Causation: *The Parent of Historical Theory*

All historians approach their study of the primary sources with some notion of how those sources fit together. In the past, some historians believed that important events always fit into an all-embracing, prearranged pattern. For example, medieval European historians saw the causes and consequences of human actions as evidence of the grand design of Divine Providence. For these chroniclers, history was God's plan for the world. Kings and princes won battles because God willed their success. More recently, some nineteenth-century American historians argued that our acquisition of a western empire was proof that God favored the expansion of the American republic. Their histories confidently offered this all-encompassing theory to explain why Native Americans had to bow before the might of European-Americans.

Most modern historians do not bind themselves in this way to an overarching, single-minded theory of causation, but content themselves with more modest conclusions about cause and effect in history. The professional historian forms hypotheses about causes and tests these against the evidence. Even the most cautious and sophisticated modern historian must ponder the connections among the groups of events and decide how these events are related.

We can classify the most common theories about causation into two large, opposite categories: materialistic theories and nonmaterialistic theories. Materialistic theories presume that the causes of human behavior over time are rooted in the material world — work, environment, natural resources, markets, nutrition, climate, and geography, for example. Most materialistic theories are deterministic; that is, their adherents argue that individuals' particular choices cannot influence or alter the grand pattern of history.

The best known of these deterministic, materialistic theories is "Scientific Marxism," first articulated by Karl Marx, a nineteenth-century economist and political theorist. Marx was appalled by the conditions of working people in industrial Germany and Britain and predicted the triumph of communism. He fully believed that the working people would gain control of the factories. He also wrote a number of historical essays to elaborate his theory of dialectical materialism. In dialectical materialism, the course of human history is determined by a struggle among different classes for control of the means of production of wealth. This struggle takes different forms as peoples pass through an inevitable sequence of historical stages: primitivism, feudalism, capitalism, and the revolution of the working people overthrowing their oppressors, finally arriving at a classless society. For Marx and those who adopted his theories, cultures and religions are flimsy structures built on the solid economic foundation of history. Individual choices within a culture cannot change the overall course of history. Some modern Marxist historians, sometimes called "Social Marxians," are not as rigid in their determinism, nor do they dismiss the importance of literature, religion, education, and culture as readily as do the Scientific Marxists.

Nonmaterialistic theories of history focus on chance rather than predetermined laws of history, stress human motives and interactions, and view change as a product of contingency (accident), human design, or irony (the unintended results of human design). The most popular, recent variety of nonmaterialistic historical theory is "psychohistory," an attempt to explain individual behavior by applying the various theories of psychology. Psychohistory emphasizes personality and personal choices as the prime causes of behavior, and has breathed new life into biographical writing.

## EXERCISE 1: *Finding Causal Statements in Your Textbook*

You already have a secondary source in your book bag — your textbook. Good textbooks heed Jefferson's command to both tell and explain our past. Find the chapter in your textbook that discusses the American Revolution. Read the section that offers explanations for the outbreak of the Revolution. In the space below, using your own words, report three of the causes your textbook's authors give for the Revolution. Decide whether each is materialistic or nonmaterialistic.

1. _____
   _____

2. _____
   _____

3. _____
   _____

# *Types of History*

Jefferson also believed that political history was the most important variety of history. Modern historical writing is no longer limited to political subjects, however. Historians today are interested in studying all manner of human experience. As a result, the secondary sources of history are far more varied now than in Jefferson's time.

Historians writing different types of history select different kinds of evidence. If an author is crafting political history, he or she will be very interested in election results, voting patterns in a legislature, and politicians' speeches, as opposed to the average age at which women gave birth for the first time. By contrast, a historian studying the changing American family will focus on childbirth and marriage statistics, and pay far less attention to what politicians did or said. The types of history flow from the types of evidence the author has chosen, and the author chooses types of evidence that fit his or her subject. Examples of some types of history and possible subjects are the following:

political history: the story of government, political leaders, electoral activities, the making of policy, and the interaction of branches of government

military history: the conduct of war, the training and behavior of armies, studies of individual soldiers, tactics and strategy; and the study of weapons

diplomatic history: the study of the relations between nations, diplomats, and ideas of diplomacy

social history: the study of ways and customs, family size, daily life, education, children, and demography (population change)

cultural history: the study of language and its uses, the arts and literature, and sport and entertainment

intellectual history: the study of ideas and great thinkers, and of religion, philosophy, and the sciences economic history: the study of how an entire system (or of any of its parts) of production and consumption works, and of markets, industry, credit, and working people at all levels of the system

## EXERCISE 2: *Identifying Types of History*

The categories of history listed are neither airtight compartments nor are they exhaustive. Where does a history of newspapers fit, for example — is it social, economic, or cultural? A history of the founding and early years of Harvard College may be political as well as social and cultural. The following brief passages exemplify types of history. Mark the type that you think best fits the passage in the space provided: P for political, M for military, D for diplomatic, S for social, C for cultural, I for Intellectual, and E for economic. Briefly explain your choices.

**A** The American Revolution worked its greatest changes in the constitutional framework of state government. Republics had replaced royal colonies. Checks and balances ensured that the power of any one political official could be curbed by other officials. Regular elections upon a very broad franchise (for that day and age) guaranteed that the people retained their sovereignty. It only remained to be seen whether thirteen small republics could find a way to become one great nation.

Type: _____ Why? _____

**B** In the revolutionary era, print culture came into its own. More people than ever before began to read newspapers, pamphlets, magazines, and books. Alma-nacs, always best-sellers, were joined by all manner of cheaply produced and widely distributed forms of popular literature.

Type: _____ Why? _____

**C** The Revolution seemed to work a fundamental change in the position and power of women. With their male kin away, women assumed responsibility for farm and family, business and trade. Although women proposed that they be given full legal rights, in fact, women did not gain such rights. Instead, they became the "angels" of the home — models of domestic virtue whose right to property was still circumscribed and whose role in public affairs was curtailed.

Type: _____ Why? _____

**D** Often, Benjamin Franklin would despair of the innocence and the arrogance of the men the Continental Congress sent to help him guide American interests through the shark-infested waters of European power politics during the Revolu-tionary War. Franklin charmed the French, carried on secret negotiations with the British, wooed the Spanish, and ensnared the Dutch in his efforts to aid his beleaguered countrymen. He did not need John Adams, fretting and complaining, at his side, and was pleased when Adams left for the Netherlands. While the pedantic New Englander and the plodding Dutch butted heads, Franklin returned to his more subtle tasks.

Type: _____ Why? _____

**E** No sooner had the Revolutionary War ended than Americans indulged in an orgy of consumerism. They bought luxury items from all over Europe and resumed purchasing goods from England as though the war had never happened. The only difference was that the English and Scottish merchants no longer extended generous credit terms; after all, the Americans were no longer part of the empire. The result was a catastrophic depression that, coupled with the devastation wrought by the war, made many Revolutionary leaders doubt that the new American nation could survive.

Type: _____ Why? _____

**F** George Washington lost most of the battles that he commanded, but still is rightly judged one of America's greatest wartime generals. He not only kept an army in being when desertion and disease could easily have destroyed it but gave a moral tone to the Revolutionary War effort. Far more than a general, Washington was what a general should be in the eyes of his officers and his men. His grave face, tall, strong body, and willingness to undergo hardship made him an inspiration to others. His combination of patience and self-discipline worked a tonic upon younger officers. He became for them a symbol of republican virtue, a symbol that would last for him and them after the guns were quiet.

Type: _____ Why? _____

**G** Thomas Jefferson and Alexander Hamilton were both students of Enlightenment philosophy, but Jefferson believed that men were naturally equal, while Hamilton thought that men were by nature unequal. This difference in their view of human nature would lead to their quarrels over a wide range of political and economic issues.

Type: _____ Why? _____

## *Thesis in Secondary Sources*

A thesis, or theme, in a secondary source is the historian's argument — the point that he or she is trying to make. Historical writing is filled with theses. The mere compilation of evidence explains nothing, for by itself a piece of evidence is not "a hard, cold something with a clear outline, and measurable pressure, like a brick."[3] Primary sources are like clay on a potter's wheel; they only take shape under the pressure of the historian's trained hands. The historian's thesis is what he or she makes out of the evidence.

### EXERCISE 3: *Identifying Historians' Theses*

Look again at the short passages in the previous exercise. On the lines below, in your own words, write what you think is each author's main point, or thesis.

A. _____

_____

B. _____

_____

C. _____

_____

D. _____

_____

E. _____

_____

F. _____

_____

G. _____

_____

# When Historians Disagree

You may have noted that at times your instructor has disagreed with portions of the textbook. Such disagreements are normal and remind you that no matter how skilled the authors or how comprehensive the coverage in the textbook, there are many other ways the authors could have told their story than the way they chose. The authors know that many subjects in American history are controversial and that historians may not agree about what happened or why it happened. When your professor and your textbook differ, they merely reflect larger differences of opinion within the community of scholars.

Disagreement among historians is like a brush fire in an overgrown woods; it makes room for new growth — new books and articles. Nevertheless, the perpetually unsettled state of historical scholarship can be disquieting. It is a rare event when historians agree that one of their number has written a definitive account. Indeed, accounts that one generation of historians regard as final are often completely revised by a new generation of historians.

With this fact in mind, some historians believe that it is impossible for historical accounts to be objective or neutral. These "relativists" argue that historians are just as much influenced by their time and place as are the people they study. All secondary sources, relativists insist, are subjective accounts colored by the historian's own bias and background. Ironically, such committed relativists still aspire to write persuasive, assured, and reliable books and articles themselves. The relativists may be right, but their claims do not mean that historians should indule their prejudices. Every historian can afford to be, in the words of intellectual historian Peter Novick, more "self-conscious about the nature of our activity."[4]

## *Rewriting History*

Without taking a position in the quarrel between relativists and their critics, we can state that a good deal of the disagreement among American historians seems to be intergenerational. Each generation of historians seems determined to dispute what previous generations of historians have written. We can gain some perspective on these disagreements by thinking about secondary sources as though they were primary sources. For example, a textbook on early American history written in 1980 can be regarded as a primary source for historians' attitudes in 1980 as well as a secondary source on the colonists' attitudes in 1774. We can then uncover patterns of disagreement among historians by asking the same question about secondary sources that we learned to ask about primary sources: how does the author's work fit into his or her own time and place?

Historians are human and are as influenced by their times as anyone else. Most modern historians are trained in universities to be professional scholars. Part of this training includes recognizing and countering their own prejudices. In earlier periods of our history, historians were not so constrained, and they expressed their points of view more openly. Today, historians still have points of view, and although their differences are muted by professional rules for scholarship, a variety of interpretation is inevitable.

A fairly extended example of historiography — the study of historical writing — may serve to illustrate how historians are historical actors whose view of the world is influenced by the times in which they live. In broad terms, it is possible to group succeeding generations of historians into "schools" of like-minded individuals who lived and worked in the same era of history.

Leading historians of the **romantic school** wrote in the mid-nineteenth century, an age when history was considered a branch of "letters," or literature. They believed that the United States was unique and special, and described how men and women in America carried out a mission to bring democracy to the wilderness. These histories feature much the same dramatic plots and florid language that characterized the fictional literature of the age.

Although the romantic historians visited collections of primary sources in the United States and in Europe, these writers were more concerned with sweeping storytelling than precise documentation. In this sense, the members of the romantic school were amateur historians. They did not teach history nor did they have advanced degrees from universities. Most of them came from solid middle-class merchant or ministerial backgrounds, and they saw the country's history mirroring the story of their own families.

Despite their popularity, the authority of the romantic historical writers was challenged by a new school of professional historians in the last decades of the nineteenth century. These younger scholars, trained in German and American universities, drafted long and copiously documented dissertations to obtain doctor of philosophy degrees (Ph.D.'s) in history, and progressed to careers as professors. Influenced by the rise of the physical sciences in Germany, England, and the United States, they regarded history as a science, capable of exacting standards of proof, rather than as a branch of literature. They and their students shared a faith that history could be truly objective. This doctrine is not widely accepted today, but the educational standard that this **scientific school** fashioned for history graduate students entrenched itself in the universities: to become a professional historian, one still has to go to graduate school, obtain a graduate degree, and write a dissertation based on exhaustive research in primary materials.

Despite their foreign travel, historians in the scientific school had a very nationalistic view of history and wrote about the rise and progress of the United States as though the "nation" were a natural, inevitable, and desirable product of every people's historical development. Each nation supposedly was different, and its history reflected the traits of its people. Within this nationalism flourished racist and sexist biases that induced some scientific historians to join the movement to restrict eastern European and Asian immigration to the United States.

When the nationalistic doctrine of historical development fed into the fires of World War I, a number of younger historians broke from the scientific school's creed and sought other explanations for Americans' conduct and beliefs. These founders of the **progressive school** announced that they had discovered the mainsprings of human motivation in economic self-interest. This group of historians committed themselves to political and economic reform as well as reform of historical ideas, and their views dominated the scholarly writing of the 1920s and 1930s.

With the approach of World War II, the cynical and dispassionate analyses of the progressive school came under attack. Some politically conservative critics of the progressive historians claimed that their writings undermined American morale by denying the virtue of the founders of the nation, a particularly damaging charge as the nation geared itself for struggle against dictatorships in Europe and Asia. During and immediately after the war, a younger generation of historians proclaimed that American history was not a tale of many warring economic interests, each seeking only its own benefit, but a story of many groups merging into one nation bound by common ideals and opportunities. These historians stressed the ways in which American consensus built a great nation, and hence have been called the **consensus school.** Although progressive ideas continued to infuse the work of some young historians in the 1940s and 1950s, consensus history dominated these decades.

The rise of the civil-rights movement and increasingly acerbic domestic protest against the Vietnam War in the 1960s influenced yet another generation of historians to seek its own theoretical orientation. In reexamining American history, these scholars found that the travails of many Americans — immigrants, women, African Americans, Native Americans, and the very poor — were minimized in the consensus version of history. The younger historians argued that disfavored groups were the victims of dominant elites, abused in the factories and denied equal treatment in the public arena. The historical writing of this **New Left school** (the Old Left was a handful of radical writers in the previous generation) retains its vitality, and many of the central ideas of the New Left, particularly the need to include minority and women's history in textbooks, have enriched every history survey course.

In recent years, the self-critical momentum of the historical profession has been maintained by feminist historians calling on the profession to recognize the contributions and the separate needs of women throughout our history. In the **feminist school,** contemporary politics and professionalism have once again combined to invigorate historical writing and to prove that historians are historical actors.

The most recent generation of historians does not show the dominance of any one doctrine, however. Indeed, older scholars have recently complained that the historical writing of younger scholars is too fragmented and diverse. One characteristic does shine through this diversity, and that is an attraction to methodological rigor and innovation. Younger historians have embraced interdisciplinary studies and boldly borrow concepts from economics, sociology, anthropology, and literary criticism. Computer printouts of data figure prominently in their work. One might call the proponents of this kind of history a **technocratic school** because its leaders are so concerned with getting the methods and the definitions of the methods right. They do not have an overarching theory of our history; in fact, they attack the very notion of such a theory. Of course, if history is any guide, the next generation of historians will cast aside the technocrats' assumptions and proclaim its own vision of our past.

None of the "schools" of history described is really as uniform or as narrowminded as we have suggested. In fact, most historians in this country are unwilling to classify themselves or to label their work, much less admit that they belong to a particular school of thought. It is only through the fine-grained textures of their arguments that we can even attempt to categorize the writing of a particular historian as belonging to a distinct school.

## EXERCISE 4: *Historians' Points of View*

Following are seven short paragraphs describing some event in the American Revolution, each representing a version of one of the seven schools described earlier. From the argument in the paragraph, identify the school to which the author belongs — romantic, scientific, progressive, consensus, New Left, feminist, or technocratic. In the space provided, explain your reasoning.

**A** The American Revolution left in its wake two sets of losers — the Tories, who had kept faith with the Empire, and the wives, mothers, sisters, and daughters who joined in the revolutionary movement. These women had contributed to the victory in many ways, running farms and businesses, rearing children, tending the wounded, and even bearing arms. When the war ended, their claims for equality were brushed aside abruptly.

Type: _____ Why? _____

_____

**B** By plotting the profitability curve of American exports against the growing indebtedness of Americans on the eve of the Revolution, one can easily explain the motives of many Revolutionaries. The data is quite complex, but sophisticated computer simulations of various possible courses of action indicate that the Revolutionaries made a sensible choice when they severed the tie with Britain.

Type: _____ Why? _____

_____

**C** Behind the Revolutionary leaders' high-toned language was a propaganda machine unparalleled in its effectiveness. Stretching from Boston to Charleston, a network of Revolutionary agitators, writers, and strong-arm men worked day and night to rouse the mass of colonists to the cause of resistance, a cause that benefited no one more than the men of wealth and influence who oiled the whole apparatus.

Type: _____ Why? _____

_____

**D** The Revolutionary movement brought together men and women from all walks of life in a common cause. They shared a set of ideas about good government and a fear of luxury, corruption, and conspiracy in high places. These shared understandings motivated them to protest and when that protest was ignored, spurred them to rebellion.

Type: _____ Why? _____

_____

**E** Throughout the American Revolution ran a spirit of patriotism and heroism, the mark of a people unparalleled in history. In their sacrifices and achievements the Revolutionaries startled the European world, bringing fear into the hearts of its selfish princes and hope into the minds of its huddled masses.

Type: _____ Why? _____

_____

**F** The germ of the notion of a great nation in the wilderness lay in the special racial characteristics of the American settlers. Theirs was the blood of hardy Anglo-Saxons, whose love of personal liberty and sense of communal responsibility went all the way back to their first settlements in the forests of Northern Europe.

Type: _____ Why? _____

_____

**G** The untold story of the American Revolution took place in the streets of cities like New York, Boston, and Philadelphia. There, workingmen and women banded together to assert their rights not only against the crown, but against local elites as well. The Revolution was thus a radical event, opening doors for the poor to see a glimpse of the power they might wield.

Type: _____ Why? _____

_____

# Logical Fallacies in History

Even when historians have tried to avoid capture by any one school of historical thought and successfully avoided the most obvious bias or impartiality in their work, they may still slip into mistakes of logic. The best historians are fallible. Some of these fallacies have been collected by David Hackett Fischer in *Historians' Fallacies: Toward a Logic of Historical Thought* (1970). Fischer's book created a sensation when it was published, not because his readers were surprised by his charges, but because he had caught so many famous historians committing logical bloopers. He catalogued hundreds of different mistakes in using evidence and setting out arguments, a few of which are so common that you should become acquainted with them:

1. the *"Baconian" fallacy*, named after Roger Bacon, a thirteenth-century English philosopher, of assuming that enough facts, piled upon each other, without some preconceived hypothesis or theory to explain them, will explain themselves; and its opposite,

2. the *fallacy of the lone fact*, in which broad statements about important events or ideas are based on a single fact or too few facts;

3. the *fallacy of tunnel history*, which isolates the historian's subject from everything going on around it, and thereby ignores the complexity of a historical subject; and its opposite,

4. the *fallacy of indiscriminate pluralism*, which takes a problem, event, or subject and broadens it beyond reason, leaving the reader confused about the scope of the historian's work;

5. the *moralistic fallacy*, in which the historian admits only those facts that uplift his or her audience and sanitize his or her account or serve some other moral purpose. All other facts are censored;

6. the *presentist fallacy*, a distant cousin to the moralistic fallacy, in which the historian is only interested in those facts that lead up to the present; dead ends, losers in war and politics, and ideas that did not prove themselves are left out of the account;

7. the *holist fallacy*, in which the historian does nothing and says nothing until he or she knows everything, a species of perfectionism that is a bad example for students who have a deadline for their papers.

## EXERCISE 5: *Identifying Historians' Fallacies*

The following brief selections illustrate some of these fallacies. Can you match the examples with the preceding list?

**A** It is impossible to know what motivated King George III to reject American compromise proposals until we know everything about his personality and the motives of his many advisors and sycophants. _____

**B** The federal Constitution was a product of hundreds of years of thinking about how governments should be run and thousands of years of experience with the failure of governments. One must add to these ideas the political compromises, economic deals, or social pressures of the men who wrote it to understand the meaning of the words "We the people" in the Preamble. _____

**C** Without Virginia's assent to the new federal Constitution, there could be no federal government. This single event made all the difference both before Virginia voted to ratify and after the state ratified the federal Constitution. Before its delegates voted, the nation had no future; after the vote, the nation's destiny was determined. _____

**D** The framers of the Constitution anticipated many modern problems, and it was their ability to anticipate these problems that made the Constitution so successful. _____

**E** Alexander Hamilton's marital infidelity; James Wilson's frantic speculation in western lands; Thomas Jefferson's barely concealed radicalism; John Adams's contempt for all moral weakness; these are the endearments of bad biography, not the stuff of good history. _____

**F** If we could be the fly on the wall at the dinner party Alexander Hamilton gave in New York City, hear him persuade Madison to compromise over the Funding and Assumption Act for the national debt, watch the reactions of the people in the room — had we all these firsthand facts, we could explain everything about the origin of the first two-party system. There is no need for theory; simple facts tracing the breakup of a great friendship are all we need to tell the story. _____

**G** When the delegates to the Philadelphia Convention met to write a constitution for the new nation, they left behind them all local biases, personal prejudices, and selfish interests. They were motivated only by the desperate straits which America faced. All else paled by comparison. _____

Historians make mistakes; historians are products of their times; historians are capable of bias, narrow-mindedness, and logical errors. All this notwithstanding, every society owes a great debt to its historians. They are the keepers of communal memory. As Carl Becker reminded us long ago, "History [is] the artificial extension of the social memory . . . [it] is an art of long standing, necessarily so since it springs instinctively from the impulse to enlarge the range of human experience."[5]

To most of us, the historian's craft appears a sedentary vocation, in which historians glide almost effortlessly about the archive or the library in search of primary sources, then sit down to write their accounts; but historians are sometimes more than guardians of our past. When tyrants or mobs suppress free expression and disinterested scholarship or demand that history lie or keep silent, then some historians become heroes. In helping all of us to remember a past at odds with the present, historians defend our liberty.

Shortly before the Nazis executed French historian Marc Bloch for his part in the resistance against them, he wrote:

> It is in time and, therefore, in history that the great drama of Sin and Redemption . . . is unfolded. Our art, our literary monuments, resound with echoes of the past. Our men of action have its real or pretended lessons incessantly on their lips. . . . It is not in itself inconceivable that our [civilization] may, one day, turn away from [its] history, and historians would do well to reflect upon this possibility. . . . .should we come to this, it would be at the cost of a serious rupture with our most unvarying intellectual traditions.[6]

Hiding from the Nazis while writing his last book, *The Historian's Craft*, Bloch lamented that he could not get to a library to check his facts. You have the opportunity that misfortune denied him, and in the next chapter you will find why Bloch, like all historians, regarded libraries as indispensable.

## NOTES

1. Simon Schama, *Dead Certainties* (New York: Knopf, 1991), 320.
2. Timothy H. Breen, *Imagining the Past: East Hampton Histories* (Reading, Mass.: Addison-Wesley, 1989), 295.
3. Carl Becker, "What Are Historical Facts?" in Phil L. Snyder, ed., *Detachment and the Writing of History: Essays and Letters of Carl L. Becker* (Ithaca, N.Y.: Cornell University Press, 1958), 45.
4. Peter Novick, *That Noble Dream: The "Objectivity Question" and the American Historical Profession* (Cambridge: Cambridge University Press, 1988), 628.
5. Carl L. Becker, "Everyman His Own Historian," *American Historical Review* 37 (1932), 236.
6. Marc Bloch, *The Historian's Craft*, tr. Peter Putnam ([1942] New York: Vintage Books, 1953), 5.

# 4 HUNTING FOR EVIDENCE: LIBRARY SKILLS

## *The Revolutionary Generation*

Historians are investigators looking for clues to understand what happened in the past. As the English historian Robin Winks has written,

> The routine [of investigation] must be pursued or the clue may be missed; the apparently false trail must be followed in order to be certain that it is false; the mute witnesses must be asked the reasons for their silence, for the piece of evidence that is missing from where one might reasonably expect to find it is, after all, a form of evidence in itself.[1]

Where do historians locate this evidence? Sometimes they travel all over the world seeking primary sources, but there is much to find closer to home, in the library. Students as well as historians can use college or local libraries to uncover and check on sources.

We live in revolutionary times — the era of the "information revolution." One easy way to cope with the information revolution is to master basic library skills. The techniques discussed in this chapter are transsubstantive — that is, you can use them to investigate topics in the humanities and social sciences as well as those assigned for this course.

Libraries have always been the great repositories of human learning and aspiration. Indeed, they are synonymous with civilization, for all great civilizations have stored their wisdom in libraries. Among the greatest tragedies in history have been the destruction or desecration of these storehouses of literature and science.

Not all libraries are comprehensive in their holdings. Some, like the Library of Congress in Washington, D.C., the New York Public Library in New York City, or the British Library in London, England, have nearly complete collections of all books and journals ever published. Some university libraries — for example, the library system of Harvard University — have collections that are nearly as extensive as the national libraries of the United States and the United Kingdom. Many smaller university, college, and regional libraries throughout the country offer excellent, if more selective, collections of books, magazines and journals, newspapers, and research aids. The descriptions and exercises that follow are based on the resources of a wide variety of college libraries visited over the past two years. If your college library does not have the particular reference books or research aids we mention, the reference librarian will help you to substitute appropriate materials. With the limitations of smaller libraries in mind, we have provided alternative selections for some exercises.

## A Tour of the Library

A typical college library includes the following locations:

1. The card catalog and, if available, computer terminals
2. The circulation desk where books are checked out
3. The reference desk and reference room or area
4. The reserve desk or room
5. The periodicals room or section
6. The "stacks" or shelves where most books are located
7. The government-documents room or area
8. Rooms housing "special collections" of primary sources
9. The interlibrary loan department
10. The microfilm and microforms reading area

Many libraries provide written guides or pamphlets for users that include a map showing rooms and areas of interest. Almost all college libraries will arrange tours for students.

# Primary Sources in the Library

Libraries contain primary sources of history in many forms. Some libraries have "special collections" of original historical documents deposited by the descendants of the authors of these documents. Almost all libraries have government-documents rooms or areas. Federal- and state-government reports, records of legislative debates, copies of the acts of legislatures and the opinions of courts, and published transcripts of the hearings of committees are examples of government documents and are primary sources. The library also has newspapers, magazines, and books published in the past — primary sources for the study of the periods in which these printed materials were written.

### EXERCISE 1: *The Card Catalog*

This exercise utilizes the card catalog or the computer-assisted search terminal to track down collections of the "papers" — letters, speeches, and writings — of historical figures. Bibliographers at the Library of Congress prepare the cards in the card catalog. The card catalog is divided into a subject index and an author/title index. The computer terminal has keys that do the same thing, although the entries in the online computer are rarely as reliable as the card catalog and often do not include older books that can be found in the card catalog.

In the card catalog, find a published collection of the papers of one of the signers of the Declaration of Independence. To assist you in sorting out the information on a catalog card, we have reproduced the card-catalog entries for the papers of George Washington in Figure 4.1. (Although a leading revolutionary, Washington did not sign the Declaration. He was commanding the Continental army on Long Island in New York on July 4, 1776). A volume like the *Papers of George Washington*

*Card #1*

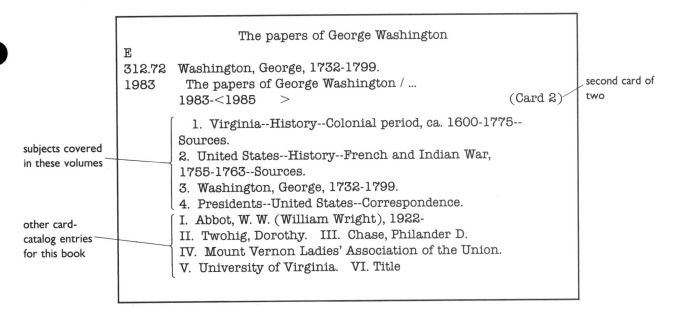

call number — where book can be found on the shelves

editors and/or authors

date(s) of publication

International Standard Book Number

identification of the library from which the card was taken (GU = University of Georgia)

The Papers of George Washington

E
312.72   Washington, George, 1732-1799.
1983        The Papers of George Washington /
              W. W. Abbot, editor, Dorothy Twohig, associate editor,
              Philander D. Chase, Beverly H. Runge, and Frederick Hall
              Schmidt, assistant editors. --
              Charlottesville  :  University Press of Virginia,
              1983-<1985     >
                 <v. A, 1-4; B, 1; in 5      >: ill. ; 25 cm.
              "Sponsored by the Mount Vernon Ladies' Association of the
              Union and the University of Virginia with the support of the
              National Endowment for the Humanities".
                 Includes bibliography and indexes.
                 ISBN 0-813-9-0912-0 (Colonial ser. :  v. 1)

GU

author
title
publisher and place of publication
height of the book
sponsors of publication
additional features
number of volumes in library so far

*Card #2*

The papers of George Washington

E
312.72   Washington, George, 1732-1799.
1983        The papers of George Washington / ...
              1983-<1985     >                                              (Card 2)

                 1. Virginia--History--Colonial period, ca. 1600-1775--
              Sources.
                 2. United States--History--French and Indian War,
              1755-1763--Sources.
                 3. Washington, George, 1732-1799.
                 4. Presidents--United States--Correspondence.
                 I. Abbot, W. W. (William Wright), 1922-
                 II. Twohig, Dorothy.   III. Chase, Philander D.
                 IV. Mount Vernon Ladies' Association of the Union.
                 V. University of Virginia.   VI. Title

second card of two

subjects covered in these volumes

other card-catalog entries for this book

**FIGURE 4.1** *Cards from the Card Catalog*

contains letters and documents — all primary sources. Modern historical editors provide extensive footnotes on the events and people mentioned in such primary sources.

Use the card catalog or the terminal to find a volume of the papers or writings of a revolutionary leader who signed the Declaration of Independence. (*Hint:* All the signers of the Declaration of Independence were revolutionary leaders, and most textbooks include in their appendixes a list of the signers.) Prepare a short list of revolutionary leaders and look in the card-catalog author section for a volume of the papers of anyone on your list. With the catalog card as your guide, write in the space following the name of your revolutionary figure the name of the editor of the papers, the full title of the volume or series of volumes, the city in which it was published, the name of the publisher, the year of publication, the number of volumes in the collection, and the call number.

_____

_____

_____

_____

## EXERCISE 2: *Using the Stacks or Shelving Area*

Library books are shelved according to various numbering systems. The Dewey decimal system is common in most public and high school libraries. College librarians prefer the Library of Congress system. Some libraries, for example, the Widener Library at Harvard University, developed their own cataloging system, but that method has given way to the Library of Congress system.

In the stacks, find the volume you described in exercise 1. Take the volume and photocopy one of the documents in it. This is your primary source. Review exercise 3: Discovering Differences in Chapter 1 and write two ways in which the habits, ideas, or behavior portrayed in the primary source you copied contrasts with modern customs and conduct.

1. _____

   _____

2. _____

   _____

## EXERCISE 3: *The Web of the Past*

Look at the date on the letter or document you have photocopied. What else was happening when that primary source was created? What might the author of your document have been thinking? Questions like these will lead you to put your primary source back into its context and to surround it with other primary sources from the same period and place. Think of the primary source as one strand in a spider's web; you want to travel from that tiny strand around the entire web.

### Option I

In the space provided, write down three clues your document gives you to the time and place in which it was written — three facts that you can discern from the original evidence in the document. (*Hint:* Choose a primary source filled with detail!)

1. _____

2. _____

3. _____

**Option 2**

If you wanted to know what was going on yesterday somewhere in the United States, you would read a newspaper. Another way to find out about the web of events and people surrounding a primary source of history is to read a newspaper from that time period. In most larger college libraries there is a microforms area where microfilms or microcards of old newspapers are kept.

Your library may have among its collection of microforms the Readex Microprint Early American Newspaper series. These are 6″ × 9″ microprint cards of the oldest American newspapers grouped alphabetically in oversized blue boxes. The series includes microform reproductions of the originals of such newspapers as James Franklin's *New-England Courant* and his younger brother Benjamin's *Pennsylvania Gazette.* Ask for help in finding this collection and select a newspaper (the contents of each box appear in white labels on the outside of the box) microcard for the geographical area closest to where your subject was when he wrote the letter or speech you copied. When removing a card from the box, put a note card or other piece of paper to mark the place. Find the issue with the date closest to the date of your primary source.

Note that our first newspapers and the newspapers today are very different. Eighteenth-century newspapers did not feature a lot of news. Half of their four or eight pages was devoted to reprinting stories from other newspapers, some of which were many months out of date. Another large portion of the pages was given over to announcements and advertisements. Finally, space was provided for letters to the editor (some of which the editor wrote) and editorials (some of which the editor borrowed from other newspapers). Find a news story in your newspaper and summarize its contents.

_____

_____

_____

## *The Reference Desk*

The reference desk at the library is the most important help station in the building. At or near the reference desk are collections of indispensable research aids — encyclopedias, glossaries, and other reference works. There are also historical reference works that list other historical reference works: Helen J. Poulton, *The Historian's Handbook: A Descriptive Guide to Reference Works* (1972); Eugene Sheehy, *Guide to Reference Works* (8th ed., 1976); and Carl M. White, *Sources of Information in the Social Sciences* (1973). For a place or date in American history, you can use Thomas H. Johnson, *The Oxford Companion to American History* (1966); Louise Ketz, ed., *Dictionary of American History*, 8 vols. (rev. ed., 1976); or Richard B. Morris, *The Encyclopedia of American History* (16th ed., 1982). Brief biographies of leading Americans appear in the many volumes of *The Dictionary of American Biography* and the four volumes of *Notable American Women.* The Hammond *United States History Atlas* is one of many sources for historical maps, as is W. Kirk Reynolds, ed., *Atlas of American History* (rev. ed., 1984).

Locating the exact research aid you need is the first step in using the reference area of the library. Almost all libraries group reference works by subject and shelve them accordingly. You can find these works by looking them up in the card catalog by title or author and then using the call number to track down the shelf location. The reference librarian will assist you in this task, as well as in deciding which research aid to use.

**EXERCISE 4:** *Using Standard Reference Works*

Using standard reference works, find the year of the births and deaths of the following Americans who became famous in the era of the Revolution.

Abigail Adams          born _____    died _____

Tecumseh              born _____    died _____

Benjamin Rush         born _____    died _____

Martha Washington     born _____    died _____

Phyllis Wheatly       born _____    died _____

Today, birth dates are common pieces of information, and most of us celebrate birthdays. In the eighteenth century, many Americans did not know their exact birth date or even their exact age. Scholars may not agree about the birth dates of famous people who lived long ago. For example, historians still debate whether Alexander Hamilton was born in 1755 or 1757.

Even when a subject's exact birth and death dates can be offered with confidence, scholars who write biographical essays for standard encyclopedias and directories may vary in their emphases and assessments of the same subject. This is particularly likely when scholarly treatments of an individual, movement, or period of history have changed markedly over time. To continue exercise 4, read the biographical entry on Tecumseh in the *Dictionary of American Biography*. This entry was written in the 1930s. Next read the entry on Tecumseh in Magill's *Great Lives From History, American Series*, published in 1987, or any other encyclopedia or biographical dictionary published after 1970. Do you find differences in tone and emphasis? In particular, are Native Americans viewed differently in the two essays? Why might this be so?

_____

_____

_____

_____

**EXERCISE 5:** *Using Reference Guides to Find Old Books*

In addition to basic reference works, the reference area has many highly specialized guides and research aids for locating old books on particular subjects. This exercise asks you to track down a particular book that was written between 1800 and 1815 and published in the United States. In those years, there was a veritable explosion of what scholars now call "print literacy." Cultural leaders in the new nation were eager to prove that Americans were capable of preserving their liberty, and widespread literacy was seen as an important part of this project. Towns and churches were expanding their support for elementary schools, and publishing firms were springing up all over the country. Peddlers carried books along with pots and tools up and down frontier trails.

One of the best sellers in this new market for American books was a biography of George Washington written by an American shortly after Washington died in 1799. Many editions followed the first, with some variation of title. Using these clues, and the information that follows, find the author's name, the title, and date and place of publication of any edition of the book, and write this information in the space provided. What famous story about young Washington originated in this book?

_____

_____

_____

If your library has it, Charles Evans, *American Bibliography: A Chronological Dictionary of All Books . . . Printed in the United States of America . . . 1639–1820* (1903; reprinted 1941) will give you immediate help. Not every library has the Evans Index or the short-title Evans Index. Your library may have Joseph Sabin, *Bibliotheca Americana: A Dictionary of Books Relating to America from Its Discovery to the Present Time* (1936). The twenty-nine volumes of this dictionary are arranged alphabetically, not by date, so you will have to trudge through it looking for publication dates. You can also use the card catalog to find your book; look under the subject, George Washington.

# Secondary Sources in the Library

Good secondary sources help you understand times and places unlike your own. They put primary sources into context, the larger picture of the people and places in which the primary source originated. The best secondary sources are also how-to manuals and models for students. You can agree with or take issue with any individual author's arguments, but able scholarship always helps you to frame your thinking. Secondary sources are an essential part of any study of history.

## *The Shapes of Secondary Sources*

Secondary sources come in many forms. They can be books, articles, parts of encyclopedias, or annotated bibliographies. They can be old or new. Sometimes a scholarly book or article published many years ago stands the test of time. Succeeding generations of scholars continue to find it provocative and instructive. Just as Beethoven's symphonies and the Beatles' "Norwegian Wood" have retained their power to entertain us, so these classics of historical writing continue to enlighten us. Nevertheless, the number of secondary sources in history is increasing at an exponential rate. To find the classics and keep track of the latest literature on any topic, you need to know where to look. As with your search for primary sources, help is at hand in the library.

Professional historians and historical editors prepare most secondary sources in history, edit and (if necessary) translate primary sources, review each other's work, direct the preservation of historical sites, manage archives and collections of historical materials, serve on local and national advisory committees, and most important of all, teach history. Historians have no monopoly on producing secondary sources, however. Journalists, political scientists, economists, anthropologists, and sociologists have all written excellent histories.

Some nonhistorians research and write for specialized audiences. For example, genealogists are researchers who receive fees to help individuals prepare genealogies, sometimes called family trees. Ancient Roman families called on genealogists to perform this service, and medieval European monks furnished genealogies for noble families. (Often the results were highly fanciful.) Modern genealogical techniques were first introduced by William Dugdale (1605–1686) of England. He insisted that every birth and death be fully authenticated and supported by scholarly references.

Local and community histories are another common secondary source. Today the curators or staff of local historical societies research and write these accounts of the origins and development of towns, counties, and regions, but in the past commercial firms specializing in such publications sold them directly to families whose names were mentioned or businesses whose buildings were pictured.

## Finding the Best Secondary Sources

You can find secondary sources on historical topics in a number of ways. Once you have found one, it will lead to others. For example, at the end of each chapter of your textbook you will see suggestions for further reading in other secondary sources. In the bibliographies of each of those books you will discover still more secondary sources on the same topic.

There are three other ways to begin a broad search for secondary sources on any topic:

1. You can use the card catalog subject index or the computer terminal subject search to look for a topic. For example, if you are looking for books on urbanization, you can also look for books on cities or, a little more imaginatively, books on particular cities. Once you have decided on a series of key words (for example, the names of particular cities), you can switch over to the title index in the card catalog or to the title search in the computer terminal. Likewise, if you want to find other books by the same author, you can use the card-catalog author index or the computer-terminal author search.

2. You can search in the stacks. Once you have found one secondary source, look at the other books around it on the shelf. Books are shelved first according to subject matter and then alphabetically by the author's last name. The books next to your book on the shelf are on the same or closely related topics. Read their bibliographies to trace the books and articles that their authors used. These bibliographies and notes refer to books and articles written before the author wrote her or his book. Not all books on your topic are shelved in the history section of the stacks. For example, you may be interested in books on the history of the first American cities. Some of your secondary sources will be shelved with the books on architecture, others with the books on urban sociology or urban literature.

3. Spadework in the stacks helps you to extend your search for secondary sources back in time, but to find the most recent works on your subject you should refer to reference aids like *America: History and Life,* a comprehensive listing of articles with brief summaries (called abstracts) of contents, and citations of reviews and doctoral dissertations. *America: History and Life* also features comprehensive indexes by author, subject, and title, covering the years 1954 to the present.

Books are not the only secondary sources you may wish to consult. For every history book on any topic there are dozens of scholarly articles in historical journals. The best way to get at recent literature on any historical subject is to use these scholarly journals. Some of them focus on particular topics — for example, *Diplomatic History, Feminist Studies,* and *The Journal of Southern History.* Others concentrate on a particular state — for example, *The Georgia Historical Quarterly* and the *Pennsylvania Magazine of History and Biography.* There are journals concerned with the methods that scholars use — for example, *The Journal of Interdisciplinary History* and *Social History.* Still other journals reserve their space for a particular period of time — for example, *Civil War History, The Journal of the Early American Republic,* and *The William and Mary Quarterly* (pre-1815 American history and culture). Lists of journals by topic and title are available in your library on microfiche and in the card catalog.

Back issues of these journals are bound by volume and kept in the stacks. Current issues are in your library periodical room.

Scholarly journals have three or four articles in each issue. Some journals have yearly indexes, but often you just have to plow through the bound issues to find something on a particular topic. The *Journal of American History* lists articles and dissertations in American history published during that year. When you have found an article on your topic, use the notes in it the same way you used the bibliography and notes in the books to widen the search for secondary sources.

## *Evaluating Secondary Sources*

Familiarity with a wide range of secondary sources is the first step in deciding which secondary sources are the most trustworthy guides. Secondary sources vary in their quality. Some books and articles are better researched and more thoughtful than others. How can you tell which secondary source is more convincing? There are *intrinsic* and *extrinsic* measures of quality. Intrinsic gauges of quality appear in the book or article itself. You do not need to go to outside authorities to use these tests. Extrinsic measures of quality require you to refer to book reviews and other published aids to assess the quality of a secondary source.

Intrinsic measures of merit include the following tests:

1. How detailed is the author's account? Does it have enough facts to satisfy an ordinary reader's curiosity? How well did the author convince *you*?
2. Does the author seem familiar with other scholars' arguments? Does he or she recognize and augment or challenge other scholars' conclusions in the text and notes?
3. Does the author use sufficient reference notes? Do the notes cite primary material or merely other secondary sources? Does the author seem to have gone directly to the primary material or relied on others' research? Do the notes seem fresh (that is, has the author made use of the most recent research on his or her topic)?
4. If your secondary source is a book, who published it? A good piece of scholarship will generally find a good publisher; that is, if the book was published by a first-rate press, you can be sure that it received a thorough review before it was accepted. Universities sponsor some of the best scholarly presses. Many leading commercial publishers also have extensive lists of history books.

At the press, editors read manuscripts that prospective authors submit, and if the manuscript passes muster it is sent out to "referees" (reviewers) — well-known and respected scholars working in the same field as the author of the manuscript. The reviewers make comments — sometimes 20–30 pages of comments — advising the press about the quality of the manuscript. The editor relays these comments to the author, who emends the manuscript accordingly. If the manuscript is accepted for publication, it undergoes copyediting and proofreading before it becomes a book.

The quality of the journal in which an article is published is a good guide to the quality of the article. The best journals send out article manuscripts to be reviewed. The author works with the journal's editor to produce the final product. A first-rate article will get published in any reputable scholarly journal. You can assess the quality of an individual article by employing the same measures you used to judge the quality of individual books.

Here are some extrinsic guides to quality secondary sources:

1. There are leading authorities in every field of historical study whose work has set the agenda for study or captured the audience in that field. Quite often, these

historians will have written books that bring together the historical writing on a topic or period. Series of such books include the New American Nation Series published by Harper Torch, the American Moment Series published by the Johns Hopkins University Press, and the American History Series published by Harlan Davidson Publishing. All of the books in these series have excellent critical bibliographies that list other books on the subject.

2. As you become familiar with a number of secondary sources on any topic, you will begin to find that some of them are cited widely. By their choice of authorities, the historians themselves are telling you which secondary sources they rate the highest.

3. Book reviews will help you to discover other scholars' evaluation of the history book you have in your hand. The reviewers restate the thesis or theme of a book, report its findings, and then assess the quality of the book and the success of the author in completing the task he or she has set out to accomplish. In your library, you will find reviews of history books in commercial periodicals like *Choice, Current Reviews for College Libraries* and *Library Journal*. These are the publications that help librarians decide which books to order. *Choice* was first published in 1963, and reviews in it can be quite incisive. An older and somewhat blander source of reviews is *Book Review Digest*. The *Digest* goes back to 1910 and, like *Choice*, has been published continuously up to the present. It offers short excerpts of reviews from many publications, including *Choice* and major scholarly journals. Like *Choice*, the *Digest* includes full bibliographical citations for books. The *Book Review Index*, which first appeared in 1965, indicates where book reviews may be found for just about every book published. The abbreviations for these sources are explained at the front of the *Index*.

More extensive reviews of books on American history appear in historical journals. The *Journal of American History* commissions reviews for just about all the serious books on American history. Many American history books are also reviewed in *The American Historical Review*. Books on early American history are reviewed in the *William and Mary Quarterly*. The essays in *Reviews in American History* are excellent extended assessments of individual books as well as specific areas of research. In addition, reviews in state and regional journals and topical journals cover books in the journal's specialty.

## EXERCISE 6: *Evaluating Secondary Sources*

This exercise helps you to formulate your own tests for evaluating secondary sources. Find a scholarly book about one of the following individuals from the generation of men and women who left their mark on the literature of the new American nation: Louisa May Alcott, James Fenimore Cooper, Nathaniel Hawthorne, Edgar Allan Poe, Harriet Beecher Stowe, or Noah Webster. Give the full citation of your book in the space provided: author, full title, publisher, place of publication, date of publication, and number of pages.

_____

_____

_____

Read the first chapter of the book and evaluate it using the intrinsic measures you have learned. We have summarized them in the following series of questions:

1. Does the author acknowledge other scholars' work? _____

_____

2. Does the author use reference notes? _____

_____

3. Does the author refer to primary sources? _____

_____

4. Do you find the author's work convincing? _____

_____

Continue the exercise by finding two reviews of your book. Indicate where you found each of your reviews. Give the reviewer's name, the title of the review, the journal or magazine in which it was published, the month and year of publication, and the page numbers.

1. _____

_____

2. _____

_____

Next, summarize the contents of the reviews. Pay particular attention to any favorable or unfavorable comments by the reviewers.

1. _____

_____

_____

_____

2. _____

_____

_____

_____

How did your intrinsic measures of the quality of the work compare with the opinions of the reviewers?

_____

_____

You began this chapter by finding primary sources and continued on to assess the quality of historians' efforts. Criticism of this sort is a necessary part of any student's education. Thus far you have been asked to find and read text. Another source of historical information that you can use in the library is maps, the subject of the next chapter.

## NOTES

1. Robin Winks, ed., *The Historian as Detective: Essays on Evidence* (New York: Harper & Row, 1968), xvii.

# 5 READING HISTORICAL MAPS: INTERPRETING VISUAL DATA

## Country and City in the New Nation

Though still in his twenties, Meriwether Lewis was not surprised when President Thomas Jefferson asked him to serve as a private secretary. Lewis had no formal education, but he was a bright, hardworking, and able officer in the army, a neighbor of Jefferson's, and soon the older statesman's confidant. Jefferson had dreamed of a great American empire stretching from the Atlantic to the Pacific, watered by the great rivers of the Northwest, and Lewis shared the dream. Even before Jefferson had arranged to purchase the vast tract known as the Louisiana Territory from France in 1803, he turned to Lewis and asked him to lead an expedition across the territory to the Pacific, mapping the features of the land. Lewis, a man of mercurial moods but vast self-confidence and great determination, leapt at the chance.

The Louisiana Purchase from France doubled the size of the United States, but few Americans had visited its endless grasslands, climbed its towering mountain ranges, or canoed along its twisting rivers. The Spanish, the French, and the British had some idea of its riches, but their maps were faulty and Jefferson knew that Americans would have to traverse the land in order to secure legal rights to the entire territory. Jefferson told Lewis that his mission was diplomatic as well as exploratory. Lewis was to negotiate with all Native Americans and Europeans he found along the way, for Jefferson had a not-so-secret goal — to ensure that the Louisiana Territory included the Pacific coast.

Lewis had seen much of the eastern United States and was a bold spirit, but he could not undertake the trip alone. He asked William Clark, the younger brother of the famous soldier and explorer George Rogers Clark, to join the expedition. Clark was a red-haired six-footer with an easygoing disposition. He could handle a boat, ride, shoot, draw a good map, and was willing to be Lewis's subordinate, though the two men agreed that the soldiers, trappers, and translators they recruited for the "voyage of discovery" were not to know about the difference in rank. Congress provided funds, Lewis spent nearly a year purchasing equipment, Clark the same time selecting the men, and after a winter of training, their long journey began in the spring of 1804.

The Lewis and Clark expedition up the Missouri, across the Continental Divide in the Rocky Mountains, and down the Columbia River to the Pacific Ocean was as epic an adventure as any Americans had ever undertaken. The explorers discovered two dozen Native American tribes and hundreds of species of birds, mammals, and flowers that no easterner had previously seen. They sent back samples of the animals and plants to Philadelphia, where painter Charles Willson Peale exhibited them in his new museum. Meanwhile, Lewis and Clark and their men (and one woman, the sixteen-year-old Shoshone Indian, Sacagawea) discovered that the Rocky Mountains were a formidable obstacle between the high prairies of the eastern plains and the lush greenery of the Pacific slope. Their expedition destroyed forever the aspiration that a water passage could be found from the Mississippi to the Pacific, for the upper reaches of the Missouri were barely navigable, and the explorers had to ride across the mountains on horseback.

Their journals describing the two years of travel were condensed and published in 1814, but the many scientific discoveries that Lewis made in botany and zoology were not published for nearly eighty years. Lewis, always moody and sometimes morose, convinced himself that hidden enemies were plotting against him. In 1809 he committed suicide. Clark distinguished himself as Indian commissioner, and his many rough drafts of maps of the northwestern parts of the Louisiana Purchase, printed with the journal of the expedition, radically altered Americans' thinking about the Far West. When Jefferson saw them, he was delighted. Lewis and Clark had done what he had asked, and the maps proved it: they had staked the United States' claim to the Pacific shore.

## EXERCISE 1: *Mapping a Wilderness*

Spanish, French, and British explorers, traders, missionaries, and soldiers had passed through portions of the Louisiana Territory and had published their maps. Jefferson read them and so did Lewis. Shown in Figure 5.1 is the last of these to appear before Lewis and Clark sailed their barge up the Missouri. This map was prepared by an American mapmaker, Nicholas King of Philadelphia. King was no explorer, but his map reflected the state of knowledge about the Northwest in 1803. Compare King's map with one showing the modern United States or North America in your textbook, and list the key features of the Far West that King omitted.

_____

_____

_____

Figure 5.2 is a reproduction of Clark's map, published in 1814. Clark had redrawn many of the sketches he had made on the expedition, put them together, and incorporated the discoveries made by trapper Zebulon Pike's expedition into the Rockies during 1806 and 1807. What are the striking differences between Clark's map and King's?

_____

_____

_____

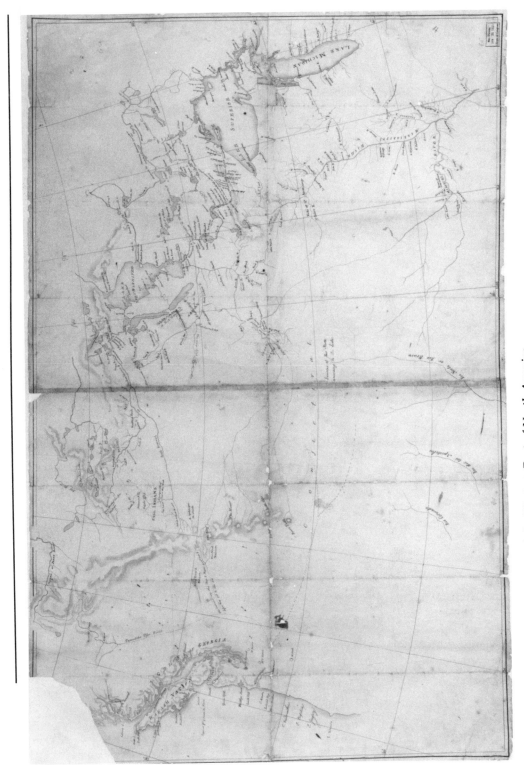

**FIGURE 5.1** *Nicholas King's 1803 Map of the Western Part of North America*

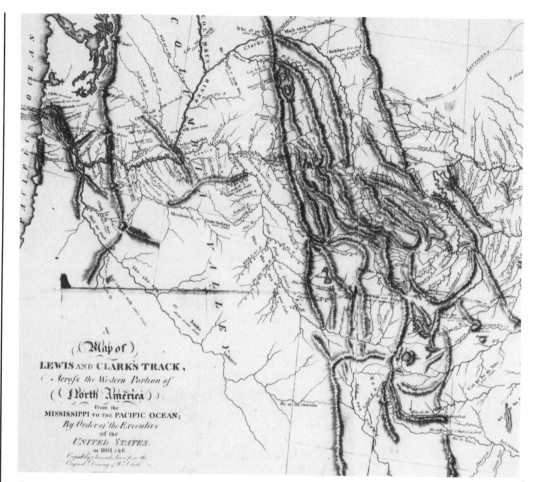

**FIGURE 5.2** *Samuel Lewis's Copy of Clark's 1810 Manuscript (Detail)*

# The Functions of Maps:
# Possession, Information, and Memory

Historically, maps perform one or more functions. The first is to claim possession of land. The second is to give directions, to guide, and incidentally or purposely to advertise places. Maps also capture a moment in time, a visual memory of where people lived, roads and rivers passed, and natural geographic features once stood.

Maps defined the land grants that European kings gave to Proprietors in the New World. Mapmakers guessed at distances and the shapes of coastlines. Explorers, traders, and settlers made their own rough maps of the edges of the North American continent. Columbus was an amateur mapmaker and used a compass and other tools to map Hispaniola and the other islands of the West Indies that he visited between 1492 and 1502. His maps, as much as the rare ores and the Native American captives he carried back with him, substantiated Spain's claims to the New World.

For the settlers themselves, maps of towns and the surrounding countryside were a visual record of who owned what piece of land. No sooner were the first British immigrants in the New World finished with their housebuilding than they took out their surveyor's tools — compasses, tripods and rods for measuring, and ruled paper — and began to lay out plats of their property. George Washington was a trained surveyor and never lost his skill; it helped him decide which parcels of land to buy for his plantation in Virginia. During the Revolutionary War he complained to the Continental Congress that he could not fight the British without better maps.

Colonial officials commissioned surveyors like Washington to make maps of the dividing lines between colonies. William Byrd of Virginia, who served on the commission that surveyed the line between North Carolina and Virginia, left two journals of his experiences. The official journal contained a map. The unofficial journal featured riotously funny gossip about the other commissioners and a thoroughly nasty description of the "lubbers" of North Carolina. When the Proprietors of Pennsylvania and Maryland could not determine the boundary line between their colonies, they sent to England for surveyors. Charles Mason and Jeremiah Dixon arrived in 1763 and spent the next four years laying out the dividing line between Pennsylvania and Maryland. Preceded by axemen to clear their field of vision and friendly Indians to give warning of raids by less-well-disposed Native Americans, the two Englishmen took measurements so precise that their accuracy has been confirmed by modern technology. In 1807 Congress established a federal program to map the coastlines, but it was not until 1879 that the U.S. Geological Survey began to make official maps of the western lands.

Clark mapped the land to lay claim to the Pacific coast in the same way that Christopher Columbus had drawn a map to claim the Caribbean islands for the King of Spain. Both men gave new names to the places they drew on their maps, ignoring many Native American names, just as they ignored most Native Americans' rights to the land. Native Americans fought over territory but did not believe that any tribe could claim absolute control over land. Jefferson and Congress, following the European legal tradition, assumed that real estate belonged to its purchaser, and the United States had paid millions of dollars to France for the Louisiana Territory.

Lewis and Clark's map did more than authenticate the new nation's right to part of the Pacific coastline. Clark's many detailed drawings indicated how Americans could go west from the Mississippi and arrive at the great Columbia River emptying into the Pacific Ocean. Later maps would fill in the details that Clark had sketched. Read alongside their extensive journals, Clark's map told fur trappers, explorers, and settlers what to expect. Indeed, on their way back from the Rockies in 1806, Lewis and Clark met the first boatloads of American fur trappers and hunters eager to follow in the expeditionaries' footsteps. In effect, the map advertised a region, opening it for enterprise — and for despoliation as well.

Finally, the Clark map captured a moment in time. It showed how the Far West appeared before the settlers came. The accompanying journals and drawings gave texture to that picture. Lewis was filled with wonder at "the immense herds of Buffaloe, deer Elk and Antelopes" that fed upon the rich grasslands. He soon learned that the game was seasonal, for his men gorged themselves when the salmon ran or when the elk herds migrated nearby, but had to survive on roots and berries when game was scarce. Maps are repositories of memory, primary sources that capture in lines and shading the way places looked in the past.

Lewis and Clark's survey had preserved a moment of time in the lives of the surveyors, the Native Americans they visited, and the animals and plants they encountered. At the same time, the Lewis and Clark mission permanently changed the high plains. No sooner had the explorers left the lower reaches of the Missouri to return to the East Coast than some Native Americans began to fall ill from diseases Lewis and Clark's men had carried with them into the mountains. The trading goods the expedition distributed altered Native American ways of hunting and dressing, particularly on the western slopes of the Rockies, the inhabitants of which had not been drawn into the European market system. The delicate balance among the tribes was permanently shifted, just as the first French explorers in Canada had shifted the balance of power between the Algonquin- and Iroquois-speaking peoples of the Northeast. The Lewis and Clark notebooks and maps became a reminder of a lost world.

# Maps as Primary Sources

In all three ways — as forms of legal documents, as guides for travelers, and as records of a moment in time — maps can be vital primary sources for historians. If a map is an original or a copy of an original, like the Clark map, it is a primary source about the ideas of mapmakers at the time and place when it was drawn. Such maps may reveal relationships among people and places that may not be so easily seen in surviving textual materials.

Historians have found maps and plans to be extraordinarily exciting primary sources. For example, when Professors Paul Boyer and Stephen Nissenbaum were preparing materials to teach their students about the Salem Witchcraft episode, they found a town map of Salem. The map, published in 1867, told them where the accusers and the accused lived. The two historians rediscovered what contemporaries no doubt knew but historians had overlooked: there was a distinct geographical grouping of accusers in the western end of the farming community of Salem Village, while the accused resided at the eastern edge of the settlement, close to Salem Town. Intrigued by the map, Boyer and Nissenbaum launched an investigation that unearthed the bitter antagonism between people in the Village whose wealth and status were on the decline and people whose ties to the Town had helped them rise up in the world. Increasingly, the Village was becoming an agricultural backwater, economically languishing and politically dependent, while the Town next to it was becoming a flourishing port. The authors concluded that jealousies and resentments originally having nothing to do with witchery fed into the terrible tragedy of the Salem witchcraft trials — a marvelous example of historical detection that began with a map.

The old map or plan must be treated as any other primary source. A map or plan reflects the state of knowledge and the value system of the person who drew it. It has a point of view and transmits a message, which the modern map reader must decode.

## EXERCISE 2: *Maps as Original Evidence*

The Pennsylvania colony was a gift from King Charles to William Penn, the son of one of Charles's loyal supporters. Penn had converted to Quakerism, a religion persecuted in England, but he was allowed to recruit fellow Quakers as settlers for his colony. Penn knew that in order to thrive the colony needed the labor of immigrants; his problem was how to induce men and women to go to the American wilderness. They not only needed directions to their new homes, they needed a reason for leaving old, familiar people and places behind.

One of the tools Penn used to advertise the colony to prospective purchasers was a map of the land between the Delaware and the Schuylkill rivers. There he proposed to build a "green country town." To these "first purchasers" Penn offered large tracts of land. He also granted to them more self-government, political rights, and civil liberties than anyone enjoyed in the mother country.

Over the years between its founding in 1682 and the outbreak of the American Revolution, the country town of Philadelphia became a city whose warehouses overflowed with goods and whose streets overflowed with people from all over the British Empire. Devastated by the Revolutionary War, Philadelphia recovered, and its ships soon plied the oceans in search of profits for its enterprising merchants.

By the 1790s, maps of the city displayed how far Philadelphia had diverged from Penn's original design. The "green country town" had become a beehive of commercial activity. The Quakers had become a minority of the population, as immigrants poured into the city from all over the British Isles and Europe. Most were poor working people — tailors, shoemakers, weavers, and laborers — attracted by dreams of improving their station in life.

There was still a sharp dividing line between city and countryside, as maps of Philadelphia in the early nineteenth century illustrate. In 1825, the city of Philadelphia was still surrounded by many independent townships. This arrangement came to an end in 1854 when the city absorbed or "incorporated" much of the countryside around it. Henceforth, Penn Township, the Northern Liberties, Spring Garden, and villages as far north as Germantown and as far south as the edge of Southwark and Passyunk, would be part of the city. By 1856, greater Philadelphia sprawled for nearly ten miles up and down the Delaware and across the Schuylkill.

The changing physical contours of the city brought new challenges and problems. Historian Sam Bass Warner has observed that "Speed, bigness, newcomers, and money beat upon settled manners with a rain of harassment and opportunity." Old community relationships within the neighborhoods of Philadelphia came apart under the strain of rapid and largely unplanned expansion of people and space. "The grid street, the narrow house lot, the row house, the interior alley, and the rear yard house or shack were endlessly repeated. When so repeated, however, they lost entirely their eighteenth-century character and took on instead that mixture of dreariness and confusion which so characterized nineteenth-century mass building." The traffic problem was nearly insurmountable, because most of the streets were too narrow to accommodate more than one carriage or cart, and the streets in the grid crossed each other too often to allow for smooth traffic flow. Factories, warehouses, and mills were scattered throughout older residential areas, further congesting traffic flow. There were few natural centers for community activities, as in New England towns.[1]

As you look at the maps in Figures 5.3 to 5.7 and read the accompanying descriptions, think about the three functions of maps: to show how land is distributed and who owns it, to guide people to and advertise places, and to capture the relationships between humans and natural features of the land. All four of the following maps exhibit these three functions. Headnotes describe each map and specific study questions follow. Answer them in the space provided.

**A** Penn had given serious attention to the design of the town of Philadelphia. He was much impressed by plans for a renovation of London after the Great Fire of 1666. The London City Council did not adopt any of these plans, but Penn did. He decided that his new town would not resemble a typical English town, with its winding streets and its haphazard development, nor would it be a teeming, crowded metropolis like London. Instead, Penn opted for geometrical symmetry and equality. His town would be laid out in a grid of square blocks with streets crossing each other at right angles from the Delaware River in the east to the Schuylkill River in the west. In Penn's plan shown in Figure 5.3, each square represented a block of land that could accommodate four or five two- or three-story

**FIGURE 5.3** *William Penn's "Plan of Pennsylvania" (Philadelphia)*

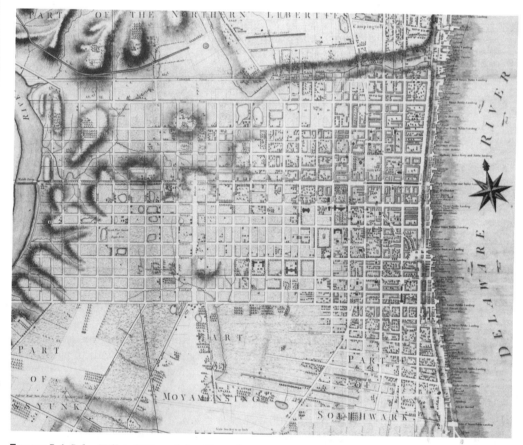

**FIGURE 5.4** *John Hills's "Plan of the City of Philadelphia," 1796*

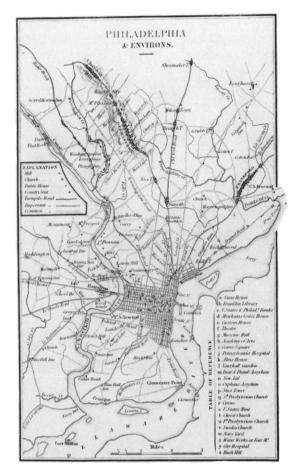

**FIGURE 5.5** *"Philadelphia and Environs"*

houses. At the back of each row of houses there was an alley, bisecting the square. In time, the rich would build coach houses on the alleys, which the poor would soon turn into crowded and dark shanties. Penn drew large gardenlike squares to bring trees and greenery into the town and prevent the spread of fires like that which consumed much of London.

1. Look at Penn's plan closely. What was the overall geometric shape of Philadelphia? _____

   _____

2. How did that shape reinforce Penn's design of the block system of lots? _____

   _____

3. Would this facilitate the selling of lots by land speculators? (*Hint:* A square contains more area than any other geometric shape with the same perimeter.)

   _____

   _____

**FIGURE 5.6** *George Lehman,* **Eastern Penitentiary of Pennsylvania** *(1833)*

4. How many main streets were there? _____

_____

5. Would a lot facing on the main streets be more valuable than one facing on a

   side street? _____

_____

6. The Quakers were often good businessmen and -women. How well was the city

   placed for commerce? _____

_____

**B** By 1796 Philadelphia was the capital of a new nation stretching from Maine
to the northern edge of Florida. The city itself had become wealthy, powerful, and
proud. John Hills, a surveyor as well as a draftsman, needed more than a square
yard of paper to complete his detailed enumeration of the public buildings and
major businesses of the Center City bounded by the Delaware and the Schuylkill
rivers on the east and west, and by Cedar and Vine Streets on the south and north.
In 1796, he dedicated the map, shown in Figure 5.4, to the mayor and aldermen of
the city and sold engraved copies to the general public.

1. What had happened to the Penn design for the city? In particular, were its
   inhabitants spreading themselves out between the two rivers as he envisioned?

_____

_____

2. Where in fact were they congregating? _____

_____

3. Why might this pattern of development characterize a port city? _____

_____

**C** By 1825 Philadelphia was a thriving city of more than 140,000 people, but its official boundaries were still limited to the original city lines from the Delaware River to the Schuylkill River, and from Cedar Street to Vine Street.

1. How is the focus of the map shown in Figure 5.5 different from the Hills map (Figure 5.4)? _____

_____

2. How does the map (Figure 5.5) suggest that Philadelphia had become a commercial center? _____

_____

3. The heavy lines are roads. What does the pattern of roads linking the city to the countryside suggest to you about the relationship between the two? _____

_____

**D** Figure 5.5 suggests that Philadelphia was extending its tendrils out into the countryside, but the sharp distinction between city and countryside is still there. That is, you can plainly see where the city ends and the country begins. Ambitious building projects like the new state penitentiary were set in rural surroundings just outside the city. You can find the site marked "Penitentiary" just east of the Schuylkill and north of the city line. The view of the penitentiary (Figure 5.6), drawn in 1833, shows the fields around it. Throughout the eastern seaboard there was a growing fascination with nature, a romantic craze to rediscover the countryside. One element of this cultural movement was criticism of cities as dirty, crime-filled, and disease-ridden.

1. What is the relationship between the back-to-nature fad and the artist's visualization of the penitentiary? _____

_____

2. What sort of building does the penitentiary resemble? _____

_____

3. What setting has the artist given the building? (*Hint:* What do you see around it?) _____

_____

**E** This final map, Figure 5.7, was drawn in 1856, after the merger of the city and the county of Philadelphia. The townships that bordered the old city had become neighborhoods within it. The new metropolis had become an industrial center, and with industry came railroads. If you look closely at the dashes you will see the railroad lines. They went in and out of the city to the north, south, and west. The railroads carried passengers in addition to freight, and for the first time

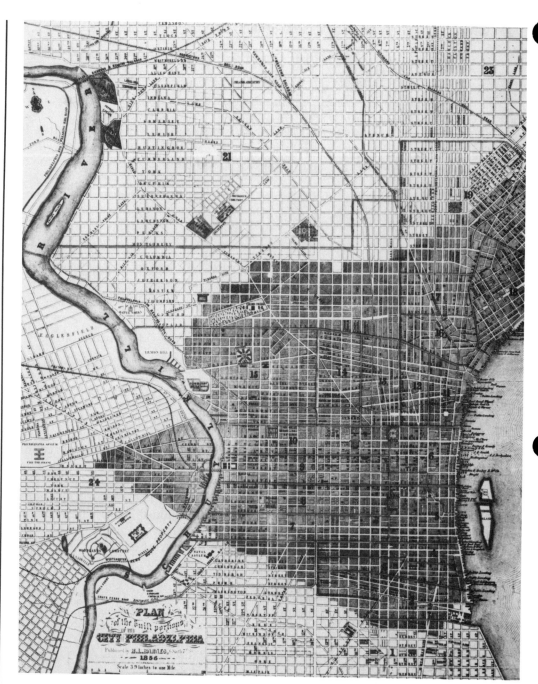

**FIGURE 5.7** *1856 Map of Philadelphia*

allowed people to live in the countryside and commute to the city to work. The number of streets had multiplied, and with them the complexity of the city. This complexity made it more difficult to get around, because there were many more streets to navigate.

1. How does your visual impression of the map in Figure 5.7 differ from the previous maps? _____

_____

2. How does it resemble a modern street map? _____

_____

3. Is the map an advertisement for the charms of the city, or is it an aid to movement
through the maze of the city streets? _____

_____

4. Does there seem to be a plan behind the city's sprawling growth? _____

_____

# Maps as Secondary Sources

You may not be accustomed to thinking about maps as secondary sources, but a
map drawn by a professional scholar to illustrate an event (a battle, for example),
a movement (the westward migration of Americans in the 1840s and 1850s, for
example), or a distribution of some sort (a map of the comparative population of
various cities, for example) is a form of argument. A modern map illustrating a
historical time is a secondary source, a tool prepared by an expert to help you
understand the geographic aspects of a historical issue or event.

Secondary-source maps became popular among historians with the rise of historical geography, the study of the effect of terrain and climate on human habitation,
at the end of the nineteenth century. Some historical geographers strongly argued
that physical setting — resources, land quality, impassable mountain barriers and
fertile valleys, navigable rivers, and jagged coastlines — provided challenges that
either aided or retarded human achievement.

By the 1910s, historians were beginning to seek the relationships between political voting patterns from place to place and other variables, such as wealth, religious
affiliation, and ethnic origin, which could also be mapped. Historian Frederick
Jackson Turner was an early proponent of the importance of geography in history
and became a prominent advocate of "analytical" mapping. In 1893 he gave a talk
at the Columbian Exposition in Chicago arguing that the vast expanse of free land
on the American frontier had shaped our unique faith in democracy and individ-
ualism. By the 1920s he had brought his commitment to historical geography to the
Huntington Library in San Marino, California. There he drew and redrew maps to
show the association between politics and economic and cultural life.

When a historian uses maps to present data and explain events, he or she is
concerned not so much with representing the geographic features — the lay of the
land — as with using these features to make a point about how or where people
lived. The map is a teaching device, not an exact representation of physical reality.
For example, in *Forging Freedom: The Formation of Philadelphia's Black Community,
1720–1840* (1988), Gary Nash presents three maps (see Figures 5.8 to 5.10) of the
residential dispersion of African-Americans in Philadelphia between 1800 and 1837
to demonstrate graphically how racial attitudes and economic forces led to the
beginnings of a ghetto.

## EXERCISE 3: *Maps as Analytical Tools*

Slaves were imported into Penn's colony from its inception, and Quaker merchants and landowners not only bought the slaves but financed the slave trade. In
the 1750s, however, the grandchildren of these Quakers experienced a crisis of

conscience. Along with non-Quaker reformers and evangelical preachers, Quaker leaders began to speak out against slavery. In 1765 there were 100 free Africans and African-Americans in Philadelphia and 1,400 slaves. By 1783 there were 1,000 free African-Americans and 400 slaves. The Revolution did not free African-Americans, despite British promises to emancipate slaves if they deserted their revolutionary masters; but afterward Pennsylvania adopted a law gradually ending slavery. Many owners went further, manumitting (freeing) their slaves immediately and unconditionally.

It remained for the freed men and women and the many African-Americans migrating to the city to find jobs, begin families, and build a community. The city attracted African-Americans seeking jobs as day laborers, servants, dock workers, street salespeople, and craftworkers. At first, freemen and -women rarely reached above lower-class occupations. Few could read or write, and their fates remained tied to the decisions of white people. Bit by bit, a small number of able African-Americans moved into the middle class. They began their own businesses and with a growing number of African-American ministers provided leadership within the African-American community.

Meanwhile, Philadelphia had become a haven for runaway slaves from Maryland and Virginia, where slavery had not been abolished. The natural increase of local African-American families also added to Philadelphia's African-American population. As the black community became more visible, white racial attitudes changed and white animosity toward African-Americans grew. Although African-Americans in the city built churches, pursued businesses, and created a thriving community that overlapped the whites' institutions, the prospect of a just multiracial society died in the early nineteenth century. As more blacks arrived, many without the skills to cope with city life, white leaders drew a color line in businesses, schools, churches, and the streets. African-Americans responded by looking within their own ranks for leadership and fashioned a distinct cultural life.

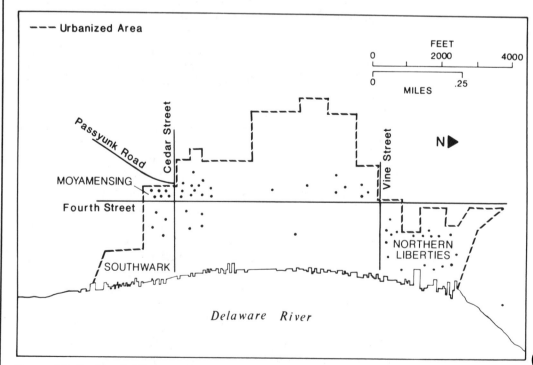

**Figure 5.8** *Residential Pattern of Black Households in Philadelphia, 1800.* One dot represents ten households.

Examine the three maps shown in Figures 5.8, 5.9, and 5.10. After each there are a series of study questions to ponder and answer.

1. Using the map legend, determine how many African-American households there were in Philadelphia in 1800. _____

2. Assuming that each household contained two parents and two children, how many Philadelphians in 1800 were African-American? _____

3. Using the Hills map in Figure 5.4, describe where these African-American families settled in relation to the central part of the city. _____

_____

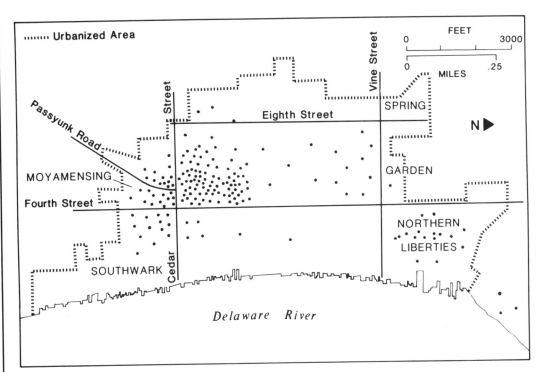

**FIGURE 5.9** *Residential Pattern of Black Households in Philadelphia, 1820.* One dot represents ten households.

1. What differences or similarities are there between the maps in Figures 5.8 and 5.9 in total African-American population and concentration or density of population? _____

_____

2. Did African-Americans distribute themselves more widely over the city between 1800 and 1820? _____

_____

Professor Nash has concluded that African-Americans were forced by their relative poverty to crowd into cheap tenements in the northern and southern sections

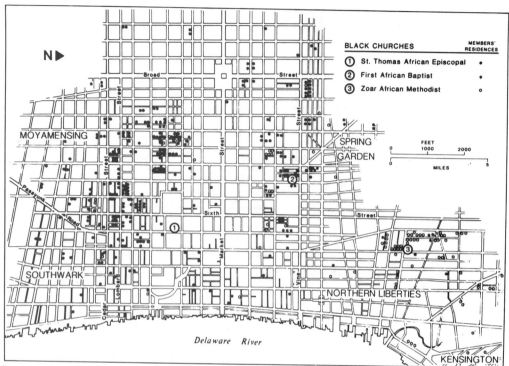

**FIGURE 5.10** *Residential Distribution of Three Black Philadelphia Congregations, 1837*

of the city. That is to say, it was not the racial prejudice of their neighbors so much as economic want that forced African-Americans to live where they did.

1. From Figure 5.10 can you discern another reason why African-Americans lived where they did? _____

_____

2. From your examination of Figure 5.10, can you reach any conclusions about the importance of African-American churches in the Philadelphia African-American community? _____

_____

Maps can be a dramatic and explicit tool for historians, an example of a picture that is worth many words. Bear in mind that such maps are arguments meant to convince you of the historian's thesis, much the same as the passages you read in Chapter 3. Such maps distort physical reality in order to make the author's point. Notice that Professor Nash has omitted many details in the first two maps, including streets. He did this deliberately, for such details would have obscured his important message — the creation of African-American communities in neighborhood living patterns. In the third map, he included streets in order to show where congregants of the three churches resided.

Even had Nash decided to re-create African-American Philadelphia in a detailed map, he would have faced obstacles. The best mapmakers must deceive us in order to inform us. As geographer Mark Monmonier reminds us, "To portray meaningful relationships for a complex, three-dimensional world on a flat sheet of paper or a video screen, a map must distort reality. . . . the map must offer a selective, incomplete view of reality. There's no escape from the cartographic paradox: to present a useful and truthful picture, an accurate map must tell white lies . . . [for] a single map is but one of an indefinitely large number of maps that might be produced for the same situation or from the same data."[2]

This chapter concludes the first half of *Reading and Writing American History* and with it our focus on reading primary and secondary sources in history. The next five chapters explore writing skills, beginning with an introduction to the basic concepts of historical writing, some tips for preparing answers to essay questions, and a section on term papers.

## NOTES

1. Sam Bass Warner, Jr., *The Private City: Philadelphia in Three Periods of its Growth* (Philadelphia: University of Pennsylvania Press, 1968), 49, 50.
2. Mark Monmonier, *How to Lie with Maps* (Chicago: University of Chicago Press, 1991), 1, 2.

# 6 THE ELEMENTS OF STYLE: OUTLINES, PARAGRAPHS, AND PAPERS

## *A Republican People and Their Politics*

Catherine Drinker Bowen would become one of the best-loved and most widely read biographers of the twentieth century, but when she was writing her first biography, she got stuck. Seeking advice, she attended a convention of historians and asked a senior professor how to write her book. He replied, "Write it from your note cards, dear." Fortunately for us, she did not stop there. Although she took copious notes and consulted them all the time, her imagination carried her beyond the pieces of cardboard in her note file. She made the people and places she wrote about live again.

As Bowen discovered, writing is never easy. The novelist James Jones, who gave us *From Here to Eternity* and other superb historical novels, once admitted that he feared and hated the blank white pages he rolled into his typewriter. The winking cursor on the word processor screen holds a similar terror for many writers today. How can you avoid writer's block, the paralysis that visits when you must tackle an essay exam, complete a theme, write a book review, or prepare a term paper?

A good general rule comes from historian Carl Becker. In 1942 he told a group of college students that the secret of his success as a writer was simple: he read and wrote constantly. Becker was right; the more you read, the better sense you have of good style. The more you write, the easier writing will become. In his youth, Benjamin Franklin wanted to write well and found models in English magazine essays. He copied these down word for word, waited a bit, then tried to rewrite them from memory. When Becker needed someone to quote to prove his point, he turned to Franklin. You are in good company if you follow their advice.

## Historical Writing: Art or Science?

Even the most famous historical writers in past centuries could not agree whether they were men of letters or scientists. The controversy is still going strong: Should historical writing be modeled on the literary essay or on the scientific report? Is written history a branch of literature or a type of science? Until the twentieth century, most historians regarded themselves as men and women of letters. At that

75

time, a literary person had considerable status in society. Thomas Babington Macaulay, perhaps the greatest stylist among nineteenth-century English historians, made a conscious decision to model his writing on the best examples of literature. His historical scholarship and his love of writing meshed perfectly and made his *History of England* one of the most admired works of literature as well as scholarship.[1]

Professor Jacques Barzun of Columbia University, a tireless modern advocate of Macaulay's position, has repeatedly warned against the dangers of regarding history as a science. He scorns "the 'theology of science' . . . [that] attracts impatient minds who fear that their free thoughts, however solidly based, will not command assent, whereas they know that the forms of science compel belief."[2] The magnetic attraction of "scientific history" worries Barzun because "the bloodless categories of classes and factors, forces and trends [characteristic of history-as-a-science writers] lack even the spare beauty of geometric figures. They are indistinct and unimaginable."[3]

Whether or not you agree with Barzun's opinions, he is quite correct that since the turn of the century the ideal of scientific precision has captivated many historians. In 1902 English historian J. B. Bury told an audience of future historical writers that "if, year by year, history is to become a more powerful force for stripping the bandages of error from the eyes of men . . . and advancing the cause of intellectual and political liberty, she will best prepare her disciples . . . by [reminding] them that . . . she is herself simply a science, no less and no more."[4]

Bury wrote at a moment in time before World War I, when some European scholars truly believed that there would be universal peace because the science of history taught statesmen how to avoid war. World War I shattered that faith, and World War II buried the broken pieces of it. Nevertheless, the dream of a scientific history still flourishes. As one modern historian recently reported, "The development of behavioral theory flowing from careful empirical studies and the refinement of statistical and mathematical models aided by modern computer technology have brought remarkable changes in the social science. These advances have convinced many historians that the marriage of science and history is now possible. At least, they argue, historical writing might become more scientific than it has been."[5]

### EXERCISE 1: *History — Story or Report?*

Undoubtedly, writing history requires artfulness of two sorts: artifice and artistry. Your bare-facts account is artificial because primary sources do not speak for themselves. You must arrange evidence into fact and fact into argument. What is more, your account must be artistic — adorned with compelling language — if it is to command the attention of a reader. At the same time, writing history also demands the attentiveness of the scientist; you must prove or disprove hypotheses with thorough and caring accuracy. Without taking sides in this debate, try this short exercise: lay any of your written history assignments alongside one of your laboratory reports and one of your English composition essays. Which of these two pieces of writing does your history piece most closely resemble? Think about it.

## Historical Prose Organization and Style

Historical writing is as varied as the skills and interests of its authors. There is no one correct way to write about a historical time or subject as there is a single correct answer to a simple algebraic problem. There are, however, some guidelines, standards, and rules that will help make your arguments clear and improve your prose style. The following suggestions will work for any kind of historical writing, from an essay examination to a full-blown research paper.

## Using an Outline

An outline can be likened to the frame of a house. There are great gaps between the studs and the crossbeams, but you can visualize what the house will look like from the framing. Before you build your house, you must have erected its frame, and before you write, you must prepare an outline. A typical outline format looks like this:

I. (Roman numeral)
   A. (Capital letters)
      1. (Arabic numbers)
         a. (lowercase letters)

The Roman numerals in the outlines will become major sections in the paper. The remaining subdivisions of the outline represent paragraphs and sentences. The capital letters introduce major topics. The Arabic numbers (1, 2, 3, . . .) are paragraphs or sentences with supporting arguments. The lowercase letters may be individual sentences or parts of sentences containing supporting evidence, illustrative details, and examples. A portion of an outline of the topic "The First American Presidential Elections" would look like this:

The First American Presidential Elections
I. The Election of George Washington, 1788
   A. Washington's place in the new nation
      1. Washington as commander-in-chief
         a. Washington as general
         b. Washington as father of his country
      2. Washington and politics before 1788
         a. Washington supports drive for national govt
         b. Washington and the Annapolis conference
         c. Washington asked to chair constitutional convention

There are four common types of outlines: chronological, topical, spatial, and biographical. In a chronological outline the argument follows the time sequence of events; your account tracks the actual occurrence of past events step by step. Chronological organization is not fancy, but it is almost always workable.

Imagine that you have been assigned an essay or face an examination question on the subject "The Rise of Democratic Politics in the United States, 1800–1836." You decide that your main points should include the election of Thomas Jefferson, the reorganization of electoral parties in the 1800s, the collapse of the Federalist party after 1815, the one-party era, the rise of Andrew Jackson, the introduction of national political conventions, and the competition between the Democratic party and the Whig party between 1832 and 1836. Each of these events can be assigned a date or chronological period. By arranging your main points according to their temporal sequence, you have begun to assemble a chronological outline.

Topical outlines are best when you are writing about an idea rather than telling a story. For example, if you were asked to write an essay or an answer to an examination question on the topic "The Idea of Democracy in the United States, 1800–1836," you might decide to focus on three key ideas — the appearance of organized opposition to people in power, the growing acceptance of freedom of speech and of the press, and the support many leaders gave to the notion of rotation in office. Because these political and legal ideas do not have exact dates, you would arrange your main points topically. You would decide which should be explored first, second, and third.

A spatial outline is best for describing a scene or an event that has a geographical dimension. An essay describing the city of Philadelphia in 1820, for example, would be best served by a spatial outline. In a spatial outline you travel from one place to another in logical order. For example, you might begin with the Delaware waterfront, move to the Center City, next describe the northern and southern "liberties," and conclude with West Philadelphia.

The last common type of outline is biographical. In it, you focus on the life of one person and organize your essay or answer around the major events in that person's life. Do not give equal weight in your outline to major events and trivial occurrences in your subject's life. You only have so much time and space — concentrate on what is important or dramatic. If you were to write about a major political figure, you might begin with that person's family and early career, use your next roman numeral to cover the person's rise to power, then continue to his or her major achievements, and finish with a section on the person's lasting influence on the politics or ideas of the time.

## EXERCISE 2: *Good Outlines Make Good Grades*

The best essay examination answers follow outlines. The question itself shapes your outline, and your outline then shapes your essay. Let us assume that you are to write an essay on the examination question: "Trace the rise to power of the Jeffersonian Republican party. What were the key events in this process?" First, read your textbook section on the party politics of the 1790s. Next, organize your thoughts and your information. In the following outline, fill in the appropriate facts from your textbook. Note that the question requires a chronological approach, so your outline is chronological.

   I. Jefferson's party appears (major topic)
      A. Jefferson and Madison oppose Hamilton's programs (supporting argument)

         1. _____ (major piece of evidence)
            a. _____ (detail or example)
         2. _____ (second major piece of evidence)
            a. _____ (detail or example)
      B. _____ (second supporting argument)
         1. _____ (major piece of evidence)
            a. _____ (detail or example)
            b. _____ (detail or example)

  II. Foreign policy crises from 1794 through 1799 embarrass the Federalists but do not drive them from power (major topic)
      A. The Jay treaty of 1795 is a major embarrassment to the Federalists (supporting argument)

         1. _____ (major piece of evidence)
            a. _____ (detail or example)

B. _____ (second supporting argument)

    1. _____ (major piece of evidence)

       a. _____ (detail or example)

III. _____ (third major topic)

  A. Jefferson and his allies build local electoral parties by 1798 (supporting argument)

    1. _____ (major piece of evidence)

       a. _____ (detail or example)

  B. The Federalists split in 1800 (second supporting argument)

  C. The election outcome of 1800 vindicates Jefferson's ideas and methods (third supporting argument)

    1. _____ (major piece of evidence)

       a. _____ (detail or example)

Every essay question suggests a structure for an outline. After reading the appropriate section of your textbook, write on separate sheets of paper a brief outline for one of the following questions:

1. What were the causes of the War of 1812? Include information on the role that party rivalry played in the coming of the war, the desire to acquire Canada and Florida, American merchants' eagerness to compete for the Caribbean market, and the war hawks' interests.

2. Which factors propelled Andrew Jackson and his party to seek power in 1824? Explore the forces that he used to aid his cause and the groups that supported him.

3. What mixture of personalities, issues, and strategies allowed the Whig party to win the presidency in 1840? Pay particular attention to the activities of Henry Clay, Martin Van Buren, Daniel Webster, and William Henry Harrison, and the role that the Panic of 1837 played in the defeat of the Democrats.

## The Workhorse of Historical Prose: The Paragraph

You are reading a paragraph at this moment. The paragraph is the true workhorse of expository writing, explaining and illustrating your arguments. Every good paragraph has a topic sentence, telling the reader what to expect. Can you spot the topic sentence in this paragraph? The topic sentence need not report everything to come, but a well-structured paragraph keeps the reader interested and informed of your intentions. Each paragraph should contain no more than one main idea.

Linkages, or transitions, within and between paragraphs enable your reader to follow your argument or understand your story. The words *by contrast, on the other hand, if . . . then . . . ,* and *but for* are common signals that a transition is coming. Transitions at the ends and beginnings of paragraphs are particularly important, because they maintain the flow of your essay from paragraph to paragraph. Such transitions should foreshadow what is to come. If each paragraph is wholly self-contained, your argument will seem disconnected and jumpy. It is the balance between new ideas, arguments, and evidence on the one hand, and linkages on the other, that keeps your prose flowing smoothly.

Macaulay was a master of transitions. He glided from a paragraph on travel in late-seventeenth-century England to one on the state of the roads, to the next on highwaymen, and so on to the dreadful state of inns in the English countryside. Every step of the way, the reader followed, never realizing the range and diversity of Macaulay's subjects or the difficulties that Macaulay had overcome in making so many complex topics so accessible. With "subtlety and care" Macaulay made each transition a simple, supple joy for his readers.[6]

## EXERCISE 3: *Choosing a Topic Sentence*

The first sentence of a well-written paragraph ordinarily announces the topic of the paragraph and tells the reader what to expect. The remaining sentences in the paragraph make supporting arguments and give evidence. In the following examples, each of the three lists of sentences come from a paragraph, but we have mixed up the order of the sentences. Select which of the five should be the topic sentence. No particular choice is absolutely right; the topic sentence you select depends on the point you want to make with your facts. For each list, circle your choice of topic sentence, and then explain your choice.

**A** Do you want a paragraph about slavery in North Carolina, economic development in the antebellum period, or landownership in the South? Choose.

1. There was not so much aristocratic pretension on the slave plantations in North Carolina as in South Carolina.
2. Slavery was spreading in North Carolina at the end of the antebellum period.
3. North Carolina economic development was retarded by the lack of good harbors.
4. Approximately two-thirds of the landowners in North Carolina had farms of less than a hundred acres.
5. Nevertheless, in favored river valleys aristocratic plantations developed.[7]

The paragraph concerns _____ .

**B** What will this paragraph emphasize about mobs that terrorized the foes of slavery? Decide on a topic sentence.

1. Their members were not lower class but middle class.
2. They met purposefully and formally.
3. The conventional anti-abolitionist mob differed markedly from mobs protesting the loss of traditional rights.
4. They wanted to preserve the status quo.
5. Sometimes they represented the establishment; sometimes they *were* the establishment.[8]

The paragraph concerns _____ .

**C** There are a number of ways to arrange the following sentences describing why Americans drank so much in the years before the Civil War. How would you begin your paragraph?

1. If Americans had wanted to drink fermented beverages, most could have afforded them, but Americans preferred whiskey to beer.

2. The stubbornness of American opposition to the whiskey tax indicates a thirst for strong drinks in the antebellum era.

3. America, it appears, was a society in which people combined high aspirations with a low motivation for fulfilling goals.

4. Drinking strong whiskey was a way to allay anxiety in this era.

5. The study of American drinking habits in the years before the Civil War reveals much about Americans' aspirations and fears.[9]

The paragraph concerns _____ .

## *The Good Sentence*

Paragraphs are composed of sentences. The best sentences are clear and easy to understand; length is not necessarily important. Great American writers like Washington Irving and William Faulkner wrote sentences that were pages long; Ernest Hemingway preferred very short sentences. Consider the following example of two sentences: "Then the creeping murderer, the octopus, steals out, slowly, softly, moving like a gray mist, pretending now to be a bit of weed, now a rock, now a lump of decaying meat while its evil goat eyes watch coldly. It oozes and flows toward a feeding crab, and as it comes close its yellow eyes burn and its body turns rosy with the pulsating color of anticipation and rage." (You can find out what happens to the crab in John Steinbeck's *Cannery Row*.) The author gets away with a very complex sentence because you can almost see the octopus slither toward its prey. Your sentences can be simple or complex, with multiple parts. You should vary the length and complexity of your sentences to keep your reader's interest. Sometimes simple is best. Sometimes the complexity of your thought can only be conveyed through complex writing. As a rule, it is bad form to address the reader directly (unless you are writing a book like *Reading and Writing American History*).

Whenever possible, write in the active voice rather than the passive voice. For example, write "John Adams had a problem. No one would listen to his ideas about government" instead of "The problem was experienced by John Adams. His ideas about government went unheard." Sometimes you cannot avoid a passive construction when the alternative is "animistic language" like "the decade witnessed the passing of an era" — as though Mr. Decade and Ms. Era crossed each other on the street.

The best expository writing features strong and descriptive verbs. Do not rely on the verb *to be*. Vary your verbs. Feel free to use dramatic verbs as well as descriptive ones. When John Adams offered, advanced, presented, proposed, submitted, or voiced his views, he grumbled, roared, pleaded, cajoled, begged, threatened, wheedled, and lectured, as well as spoke or declared. Avoid clichés — phrases that are overused and easily misunderstood.

Sentences are strings of words. The English language has more than eight million words, many of them borrowed from other languages. You need not know them all to be an effective writer. William Shakespeare used only 50,000 different words to delight and entertain four centuries of English-speaking people. Although your dictionary probably includes jargon (technical terms or very specialized, generally unfamiliar words) and slang (colloquial or street language), we urge you to avoid such words.

"Weasel words" are catchall words or terms that usurp the place of stronger, more precise language. The most common weasel words, *thing, field, sector, area, factor*, and *aspect*, have precise meanings of their own. A thing is an inanimate object; a field may be plowed; a sector is a part of a map or plan; an area is a measure of two-dimensional space; a factor is a commercial agent or a mathematical operator; and an aspect is the appearance or demeanor of an object or a person. These words should not replace more precise ones.

Do not make up new words. Avoid words ending in *-ize* such as *finalize* and *initialize*. Use *finish* and *begin* instead. Do not add *-wise* to the ends of your nouns. Do not overuse weak connectors like *however* and *nevertheless*, and remember that *while* and *since* denote duration of time. Use *because* when you want to explain causation. Finally, avoid contractions; do not use *don't* in formal writing.

Correct English usage is a joy to read, but not much fun to master. Here are some common stumpers *adapted* (made to fit), not *adopted* (taken exactly as is), from Walter Sullivan and George Core's delightful *Writing from the Inside* (1983):

An *allusion* is a reference to a fact or a person; an *illusion* is a false impression.

An *alternate* is a substitute; an *alternative* is a choice.

*Blatant* means loud and obvious; *flagrant* means rude and obnoxious.

To *compose* is to create; to *comprise* is to include or contain.

*Continual* means regularly, at set periods; *continuous* means incessantly, without respite.

*Disinterested* means neutral; *uninterested* means not interested.

*Eminent* suggests respectability and esteem; *imminent* suggests immediately forthcoming.

*Exceedingly* means extremely; *excessively* means beyond any acceptable limit.

*Farther* is used with distances; *further* is used with degree of effort.

A *feasible* project is one you can accomplish; a *possible* project is one you might accomplish.

To *imply* means to suggest; to *infer* means to deduce.

*Oral* means spoken; *verbal* means relating to words.

To *precede* means to come before; to *proceed* means to go on or to advance.

*Sensual* means lewd; *sensuous* means appealing to the senses.

For more on prose style, consult the latest edition of E. B. White and William Strunk, *The Elements of Style* (1979) or H. W. Fowler's *Modern English Usage* (1983). In the end, your prose style will be unique because you are unique, but it will not convey your message if you slip into errors of usage, grammar, or tone.

## EXERCISE 4: *Pick a Sentence, Any Sentence. . . .*

The following short samples demonstrate the power of superb historical writing. You feel empathy for the characters described, because the prose puts you alongside them. Read each passage, paying special attention to the structure of sentences and the choice of words. What emotions and ideas do the authors evoke? Return to the passages and find the words or phrases that most touched your feelings. Note that here you have returned to secondary sources, but you are concerned not so much with argument (as in Chapter 3) or with quality of scholarship (as in Chapter 4) as with effectiveness of prose style.

**A** Martha Ballard was a pioneer woman, but she never went west. She lived on the Kennebec River, in Maine, bore nine children and buried three of them, was a midwife and nurse, prepared and dispensed folk remedies, and in the dead of winter crossed the dangerous ice whenever a neighbor called for aid. Born in 1735, she began a remarkable diary in 1785 and kept at it until her death in 1812. The diary is the basis for Laurel Thatcher Ulrich's prize-winning book, *A Midwife's Tale* (1990), from which this excerpt is taken. Ballard has crossed the icy river to deliver Mrs. Byrnes's twins.

> Characteristically, the one obstetrical comment in the [diary] entry ("There was but a short space between the Births") is embedded in seemingly extraneous references to the weather, her journey, the names of the men who assisted her across the river and of the women who sat up with her through the night. The biological event fades into the clutter of social detail. Where is the center of the picture? Is it Martha Ballard scrambling up the icy bank, Mr. Dingley grasping one arm, Mr. Graves reaching toward her from above, while [her husband] Ephraim slowly turns his boat in the ice-rimmed river below? Is it Mrs. Byrnes, exhausted from her eight-hour labor, bearing down for the second delivery? Is it Mrs. Conry easing two perfect babies into the cradle, or the three drowsy women leaning toward the kitchen fire, the midnight cold at their backs, small clouds of mist above their whispers? There is no center, only a kind of grid, faint trails of experience converging and deflecting across a single day.[10]

Which words or phrases struck you as powerful? Why? _____

_____

_____

**B** Women did not always stay close to home. They moved about the country, sometimes with their families, on other occasions seeking jobs and education on their own. Angelina Grimké, disgusted with slavery, left her wealthy and powerful family in Charleston, South Carolina, to seek a meaningful life in the North. There she met the future author of *Uncle Tom's Cabin*, Harriet Beecher. Their afternoon together is retold in Gerda Lerner's *The Grimké Sisters from South Carolina* (1971).

> The two young women chatted and walked on the lawns of the Hartford Female Academy. Harriet, shy and moody, but blessed with a keen sense of humor, may have smiled inwardly at this graceful Southern lady in her unbecoming Quaker bonnet who worked so zealously at self-improvement and admired the accomplishment of any schoolgirl who could rattle off a few memorized facts. . . . But that between the two of them they were destined to furnish much of the intellectual ammunition which equipped a generation of Northerners to accept the necessity for civil war, would have seemed a preposterous thought to them both. . . . Harriet, as yet quite unconcerned about slavery, questioned the one woman from whom she might have drawn authoritative information on the subject, about the odd habits and customs of Quakers . . . And Angelina, liking [Harriet], thought her rather unimpressive but sweet. They chatted pleasantly, and that was all.[11]

Which words or phrases struck you as powerful? Why?_____

_____

_____

# Term Papers and Research Papers

History is taught in almost every conceivable setting in modern colleges and universities, from the intimate discussion group to the giant lecture hall. The vast majority of students in introductory history courses do not have the opportunity to write term papers or research papers. The concluding pages are directed to those students who face the daunting but rewarding prospect of carrying out such an assignment.

To write well on any historical subject, whether you are writing an essay answer for an exam or a full-fledged term paper, you must first know your subject. Students who are having trouble starting to write will often discover that they are not yet masters of all their material. More study or outside reading on the topic will solve that problem.

## Thinking and Doing Research and Writing

In the midst of writing his famous history of England, Macaulay reported that he was always busy "thinking" and "doing." Like Macaulay, you have to think about your paper as a whole. Ask yourself what you want readers to learn from it. A good method for focusing your thoughts is to try to write down your theme or argument in no more than four lines. You must think through your arguments and plan how to prove each of them.

When Macaulay said that he was busy "doing," he did not mean only writing. Instead, he was constantly arranging and rearranging his evidence. Once you have enough evidence from primary and secondary sources to begin to see the general outline of your arguments, you can design a master plan for your paper. As you frame your master plan, continue to ask yourself whether you have enough material from your sources to support your arguments. Remember, writing and reading should loop around each other. Writing guides and directs further research. Do not hesitate to go back to the library to fill in gaps in your research that your writing reveals; then fill in those gaps with additions to your master plan.

## Research

Your research will take you to libraries and archives. You have already familiarized yourself with libraries. Archives are buildings or parts of buildings that house collections of primary sources, and that come in all shapes and sizes. The archive that houses United States documents, including the Declaration of Independence and the Constitution, is the National Archives in Washington, D.C. This giant rectangular building on the mall has two entrances. Every day thousands of Americans and foreign guests walk through the display area in the front of the building to view our Declaration of Independence and our Constitution. Thousands of researchers use the rear doors to spend the day reading and taking notes on millions of documents relating to diplomacy, government, war, and politics. The Library of Congress complex is located behind the Capitol. The ornate Jefferson building, shown in Figure 6.1, is a beautiful library containing almost every book ever published. The more functional Madison building across the street houses the papers of many famous and not-so-famous Americans in its special collections.

Not every archive is as spacious or imposing as the National Archives or the Library of Congress. In every state and many cities in our country there are historical societies and libraries that house collections of historical documents. The *Library of Congress Guide to Manuscript Collections* lists these, as well as collections of papers and manuscripts left to archives.

Archives collect and preserve two kinds of materials — public documents and private papers. Government archives like the State Archives of North Carolina in Raleigh or the State Library in Trenton, New Jersey, are the repositories for official state court records, legislative papers, and government-agency minutes and orders. State archives may also house private papers — letters, account books, family

**FIGURE 6.1** *Interior of the Jefferson Building of the Library of Congress*

records, and similar primary sources. State and local historical societies are repositories of correspondence, diaries, account books, and unpublished writings. Sometimes the sources are famous men and women, sometimes less well-known people whose papers were lovingly preserved by their descendants and given to the historical society. "Keep every scrap of paper," Abraham Lincoln's secretary John Nicolay wrote to Lincoln's only surviving child, Robert Lincoln, "Everything is priceless." Every archivist will tell you that Nicolay was right.

## *Taking Notes from Your Sources*

Whether you find your primary and secondary sources at the library or the archive, you have to take notes. Traditionally, scholars copied original documents longhand, word for word. Some, like biographer Barbara Tuchman, used 4 × 6 note cards; others, like Milton Lomask, used sheets of 8½ × 11-inch paper. With the advent of modern photocopying methods, many scholars now prefer to ask the library or archive staff to photocopy primary sources. Some primary sources cannot be photocopied (the light and heat of the machine will destroy the document), but some archives will photograph the document and sell the microfilm. Most secondary sources can be photocopied, but the cost can become prohibitive.

Let us assume you decide to copy your sources on note cards. For each source you use, prepare a bibliography card. On this card, write the exact title of the source, including the name of the collection in which it appears and the archive or library where you found it. If the source is published, write a full bibliographical citation. Keep your bibliography cards together. Each note card you use for transcribing quotes should have its own heading giving an abbreviated description of the source's title or the name of the collection and the particular source you are quoting. Remember to include page numbers for your quotes if the source is printed. *Only use one side of the note card.* If your document or quote requires more space, use additional note cards. Number the note cards consecutively. After copying the source onto the note card, check word for word to be sure there is no error.

Keep your note cards in a small box or closed bag. When the number of your note cards begins to swell, sort them by topic, author, date, event, or the place they will go in your paper. Put all cards in the same category in an envelope, file folder, note card box, or bundle.

You may want to take notes from some sources without copying them word for word. Head the note card the same way you would if you were copying the entire document or letter. Then, in your own words, summarize the gist of the source. This method is useful when you want to retain the important parts of a long document or take notes from a book or article. On the note card, quote only those passages that best represent the author's thoughts or are presented in the most dramatic or colorful language. Always include the page numbers when you have quoted or paraphrased from a printed source. Recheck your quotations to make sure they are correct.

A word to the wise: the most exasperating experience for a reader or researcher is recalling something important in a primary source but forgetting where you saw it. There is no way to prevent this from happening occasionally, but the best rule is: when in doubt, take a note. Carry extra note cards around with you for this purpose. The corollary to this rule is equally important: when you take a note, take down a full citation. A citation is a record of the source of your note. You do not want to repeat an archival search to find the origin of a quotation you already have. Good examples and good advice for note takers abound in Neil R. Stout, *Getting the Most Out of Your U.S. History Course: The History Student's Vade Mecum* (1993) and Donald J. D. Mulkerne and Donald J. D. Mulkerne, Jr., *The Perfect Term Paper: Step by Step* (1988).

You may also want to keep a research diary, which not only helps preserve a record of everything you saw but is a good place to jot down ideas for future research or notes for writing your theme or paper. Buy a spiral binder, and each day you go to the library or the archive start a new page in the diary. Label it with the date, the assignment, the library or archive you are visiting, and the collections you are using. Every time you copy a document or ask the archivist to copy a document, make a brief descriptive note in your diary. Some historians not only keep their diary entries in a spiral notebook, but also copy the primary sources into the notebook as well.

## EXERCISE 5: *Taking Notes*

This exercise will give you practice in transferring information from your sources to note cards or notebooks. The following reading selections concern the political contest that arose early in the nineteenth century between eastern and western regions of two southern states. Later, such intrastate rivalries would be overshadowed by the struggle between the North and the South, but until the 1830s the struggle between the older, better-established eastern, coastal areas and newer, poorer western regions within states dictated political alignments. At stake was political power—which region would control state government. Control of state government led directly to economic advantages. State government decided who paid taxes, where new bridges and roads were built, and which localities would be commercially developed. Read each selection and the instructions that follow to complete the exercise.

A. While the contest for the presidency occupied the attention of North Carolina's political elite during the 1820s and 1830s, a substantial portion of their constituents remained indifferent. Only 40 percent of the eligible voters participated in the presidential election of 1824, and the proportion of voters declined to a mere 30 percent in 1832. The explanation for this widespread disinterest can be found, in large part, in the irrelevance of the incipient [national political] parties to the local concerns of the electorate. Oriented exclusively toward winning control of the presidency, the leaders of the contending factions failed to address important state issues like constitutional reform and internal improvements. Indeed, these issues divided the political elite along sectional rather than artisan lines, and their constant agitation during the 1820s and 1830s threatened the development of stable political parties. Not until the Constitutional Convention of 1835 had resolved the most fundamental differences between the sections did a viable party system emerge in North Carolina.[12]

Underline the words and phrases in the passage that you think are most important. Next, using your own words, write three complete, grammatically correct sentences summarizing the author's main point. Be brief; accustom yourself to recording a lot of information with few words. We have put a heading on the note card for you.

Thomas E. Jeffrey, *State Parties and National Politics, North Carolina, 1815–1861* (Athens, Ga.: University of Georgia Press, 1989), p. 49

B. In 1809, when Jefferson stepped down from the presidency and retired to private life on his beloved mountaintop, the divisive feelings of sectionalism had replaced the harmonious, enlightened tone of the Virginia he had known and loved as a young man. In his early manhood Jefferson had seen no real social or economic conflicts in the Old Dominion, and certainly none along geographic lines. To be sure, when the delegates had gathered in the spring of 1776 at Williamsburg, a temporary geopolitical division had surfaced . . . and these . . . reflected important contrasts in patterns of mobility and landholding in the older and the newer counties during the mid-eighteenth century. But these factions proved fragile when tested in the debates on drafting the new frame of government. The result was a constitution that . . . merely "strengthened the grasp of the provincial oligarchy on the politics of the state." But a generation later the consensus had evaporated. By then a sizable number of yeomen farmers and artisans had settled the Shenandoah Valley and beyond into the

Allegheny Mountains. East of the Blue Ridge, though, things remained largely un-changed. So, by the first decades of the nineteenth century, Virginians were speaking in terms of sectional controversy, of East versus West.[13]

Again, underline the key words or phrases, then summarize the argument on the note card below.

---

Robert P. Sutton, *Revolution to Secession: Constitution Making in the Old Dominion* (Charlottesville, Va.: University of Virginia Press, 1989), p. 52

_____

_____

_____

_____

_____

_____

---

# First, Second, and Final Drafts

Let us assume that you have done enough research to begin writing. Your tentative outline, your note cards, and your bibliography cards are at hand. You have allowed yourself enough time and space to begin, and have found a quiet place in which to work. It is time for a first draft.

Some researchers prefer to wait until they have finished all their reading before starting to write. Charles Tilly, one of the foremost historians of early modern history, reminds his students to be on the lookout for additional "links in the chain of evidence." Tilly wants his students to ask themselves if they can improve their account by adding one more person, place, or thing. Tilly's advice is priceless. For example, if you are writing about labor unrest in England and the United States during the 1830s, you should ask yourself whether your account would be stronger if you also looked at anti-Catholic mobs in the same era. If you find that the additional links would not help to explain the main topic, then the chain has extended far enough, and your research is complete.

A few historians took this rule to an extreme. For example, the late Frederick Jackson Turner, one of the most forceful thinkers among early twentieth-century historians, could never bring himself to write his definitive book on the relationship between the different sections of the United States before the Civil War. He always had more evidence to collect and more maps to draw. His dedication to complete-ness consumed him (an example of the holistic fallacy you encountered in Chapter 3) and cost his readers a very good, if not perfect, book.

Other researchers do not delay writing. As the late English historian Edward Hallett Carr admonished his readers:

The commonest assumption appears to be that the historian divides [the] work into two sharply distinguishable phases or periods. First, [he or she] spends a long preliminary period reading . . . sources and filling . . . notebooks with fact: then, when this is over, [he or she] puts away [the] sources, takes out [the] notebooks, and writes . . . from beginning to end. This is to me an unconvincing and implausible picture. For myself, as soon as I have got going on a few of what I take to be the capital sources, the itch becomes too strong and I begin to write — not necessarily at the beginning, but somewhere, anywhere. Thereafter, reading and writing go on simultaneously. The writing is added to, subtracted from, re-shaped, cancelled, as I go on reading. The reading is guided and directed and made fruitful by the writing: the more I write, the more I know what I am looking for, the better I understand the significance and relevance of what I find."[14]

Whether you wait until all your research is done, or begin writing as soon as you have something to say, be mindful that everything you write is a reflection on you. Neatness counts. For your first draft, use standard size (8½ × 11-inch) ruled paper (if you are writing the draft by hand) or bond (if you are typing or using a word processor). Double-space to leave room for insertions or corrections. Keep a dictionary and thesaurus handy. Do not worry if your first draft is longer than the assignment. It is easier to cut than to add. Tell your story from beginning to end. If you are blocked at a particular point, simply go beyond it. You can always return to a difficult passage or idea later. Put in all the quotations you are going to use. Alongside the quotation, at the bottom of the page, or on a separate sheet of paper, write down the full citation for each quotation you use for protection in the event that a note card is lost or mutilated. (See the next section for the rules of quoting and citing quotations.) Make a copy of your finished draft and lay it aside for a day or two.

When you come back to your first draft you may be disappointed that your writing is not as crisp or as colorful as you remembered — first drafts are always disappointing to authors. Reread your text with the following questions in mind:

1. Did I make my points clear? Can another reader fully and immediately understand what I meant?
2. Does my paper have a beginning, a middle, and an end? Do I need to reorganize my arguments so that they flow smoothly from one to another?
3. Do I have enough evidence to support my arguments or illustrate my points?
4. Is my style fluid and my grammar correct? Would another reader enjoy my paper?
5. Have I properly used formal scholarly apparatus, quoting and citing according to the rules?
6. Have I made a real contribution on my topic? Do I seem to know what I am doing? Am I proud of my work?

In your second draft, revise the paper to respond to the questions you asked yourself. Do not hesitate to return to the library or archive, prepare new note cards, or seek advice from your instructor on difficulties. The second draft is still a working copy, but it should resemble the finished product. Have someone whose judgment you trust read your second draft after you have finished it. If your instructor offers to read second drafts, take advantage of the offer. Listen to criticism and further revise the paper if necessary. Make copies of every draft you submit.

Your third or "clean" version is the paper on which you will be graded. It should be neat and presentable. Type or print out your final paper double-spaced. Use 1-inch margins at the top, bottom, and sides of the paper. Number every page except the title page. Recheck your paper for spelling or factual errors. Hand it in with pride.

# Quoting and Citing the Words of Others

Whether you are writing a theme, a book review, or a longer research paper, some of the words you use will be taken from your sources. When you copy words or ideas from primary or secondary sources, you must give credit to your source; otherwise you are guilty of plagiarism. Plagiarism is both cheating and theft, and offenders will always be punished severely. Your student handbook describes your school's rules on this offense, but take our advice: *never do it.*

When using others' words or ideas, you may quote or paraphrase. A quotation is word-for-word borrowing. When should you quote? You may quote in order to prove a point you are making. The best proof will often be the words used in the source. Although this kind of quotation may be quite long (a "block" quotation), you should not quote any more of your source than you have to in order to prove your point. Long quotations tend to weary the reader. You also quote when you cannot say it better in your own words. You may quote short passages to enhance your own account; quotations of this sort are best merged into your writing a few words or sentences at a time.

The best term papers are those that bear the stamp of your own thinking and style. When one of the authors of this book was in middle school, his brother, then a college junior, returned home for the Thanksgiving Day holiday and announced that he had to submit a fifty-page history paper the following Monday. He then smiled and continued, "Don't worry. I'll find three or four books on the subject and quote whole pages from them. That should take up half the assignment. The rest I can make up myself." Can you guess the grade he received when he turned in his work? Do not submit a paper that is little more than a string of quotations.

Enclose all direct quotations in quotation marks (" "). If there is a quotation within the quotation (quoting an author who is quoting someone else), use single quotation marks inside the double quotation marks ("' ' "). If your quotation is longer than five lines, set it off as a separate block of text. Indent five spaces on both margins. Do not use quotation marks at the beginning or end of block quotations.

If you have left out a word, phrase, or any other material from a quotation use three dots (. . .), an "ellipsis," to show the omission. If the missing material includes a period, add that to the ellipsis (. . . .) Do not leave out material that would change the meaning of the quotation. This is often done in advertisements for movies and books. The reviewer may have said "The *Purple People Eaters* is the most terrible movie I have ever seen," but the ad says "The *Purple People Eaters* is the most." When you quote, be fair to the spirit as well as the words of the author. You may add material to a quotation to explain a term in it or correct the author's error if you put your comments in brackets ([ ]).

You may decide not to use a direct quotation but to rephrase what the source says and report it in your own words. Paraphrasing is perfectly legitimate scholarship. You can reduce a long quotation to a short paraphrase or capture the essence of a description or a conversation in a paraphrase. As in direct quotation, be sure that your paraphrase reflects the spirit of your source, and always cite its source.

# Reference Notes

Whether you quote or paraphrase, you must give credit to your source. In historical writing, you use a "reference citation" to give credit. These can be placed at the bottom of the page (a "footnote") or at the end of the paper (an "endnote"). Reference notes or citations are signaled in the text of your paper by a raised number, as the authors of this book have done. Each citation should contain the name of the author or editor, the title of the work, the publisher and place of publication, the date, and the pages quoted or cited. It should look like this:

1. Arthur M. Schlesinger, Jr., *The Age of Jackson* (Boston: Little, Brown and Co., 1945) p. (or pp. if more than one page or inclusive pages)

If an article, include the title of the article and the title of the journal or magazine in which it appeared, and the volume number of the journal or magazine. A note to an article in a journal would look like this:

1. John Lauritz Larson, "'Bind the Republic Together': The National Union and the Struggle for a System of Internal Improvements," *The Journal of American History* 74 (September 1987), p. (or pp., if more than one page)

If the work is in manuscript, include the author's name, the name of the recipient (if a letter), the date of the writing, the name of the collection in which you found the manuscript, the name of the archive or library where it is kept, and the page number if it has one:

1. Frederick Douglass to William Lloyd Garrison, February 26, 1846, Frederick Douglass Papers, Yale University Library, New Haven, Conn.

A citation to a primary source that is published combines the forms for manuscript and published works:

1. Frederick Douglass, "The Southern Style of Preaching to Slaves, January 28, 1842" in John W. Blassingame, et al., eds., *The Frederick Douglass Papers* (New Haven: Yale University Press, 1979–   ), 1:17.

Note that the Douglass talk is in Volume 1 of his published papers but that there are additional volumes. When using a primary source cited in a secondary source or published in a collection, always give the full citation of the secondary source.

The ruling concept behind citations is to give anyone else using just your reference note enough information to find the exact words you read and quoted. There have been cases in which fine historians were sloppy in their reference notes, and minor errors in the notes — errors that did not weaken the argument in the body of the work — called the entire book or article into question.

## Explanatory Notes

You may want to include in a footnote or an endnote material that explains, amplifies, or examines additional evidence about a point you have made in the text of your paper. Use an "explanatory note" to do this. The explanatory note may include references to one or more primary or secondary sources. These are usually enclosed in parentheses. The end result can look like a mini-paper. At one time, authors gave separate numbers or symbols for these explanatory notes, but now it is the custom to mix them in with the reference notes.

How many notes do you need? There is no set rule. You must provide a citation for every direct quotation and paraphrase, but note numbers for these may appear throughout the text or merely at the end of each paragraph. The former method helps the reader to find every reference but clutters your paragraphs with numbers. The block-citation method, in which all references that appear in a paragraph are given in a single citation, signaled by one note number at the end of the paragraph, is more common than the multiple-citation form. It is easier and less distracting to block-cite, but an author can hide holes in his or her evidence in block cites more easily than in individual references. If you are asked to write a research paper for your course, your instructor may indicate a preference for individual or block citations. Manuals that offer models for citation include Kate L. Turabian, *Student's Guide for Writing College Papers* (5th ed., 1987) and James D. Lester, *Writing Research Papers: A Complete Guide* (4th ed., 1984).

## *If You Use a Word Processor*

We strongly recommend that you use a word processor to write your papers. Alterations, additions, and final preparation are much easier on a word processor than on a typewriter. Each software program has its own rules, and to learn them may require a bit of effort. Once you have mastered the rudiments, you will never want to go back to the typewriter. Modern word processing programs use either function keys or a "mouse" to format the paper and deliver the program's special functions. Both systems have their passionate advocates. Use a program that allows you to add or delete footnotes automatically. Of these, Microsoft Word and WordPerfect are the two most popular programs on the market. Versions of both are made for Apple and IBM-compatible operating systems.

To write well, you must read much and write often. There are no shortcuts to good writing. In the following chapters, we will expand on the lessons of this chapter. You will have the opportunity to narrate the story of the young people who went west, analyze the relationship between slavery and wealth in the South, probe the lives of the men and women who faced the Civil War, and explore the perennial issue of the moral lessons of history.

## NOTES

1. I have taken this account from John Clive, *Macaulay: The Shaping of the Historian* (New York: Random House, 1973), 476.

2. Jacques Barzun, *Clio and the Doctors* (Chicago: University of Chicago Press, 1974), 155.

3. Ibid., 157.

4. J. B. Bury, "The Science of History" inaugural lecture as Regius Professor of Modern History, Cambridge University, 1902, reprinted in Fritz Stern, ed., *The Varieties of History* (New York: Meridian Books, 1956), 223.

5. Harold D. Woodman, "Economics and Scientific History," *Journal of Interdisciplinary History* 5 (1974), 295.

6. John Clive, *Not By Fact Alone: Essays on the Writing and Reading of History* (Boston: Houghton Mifflin, 1989), 20.

7. Adapted from Clement Eaton, *The Growth of Southern Civilization, 1790–1860* (New York: Harper & Row, 1961), 185.

8. Adapted from Leonard L. Richards, *Gentlemen of Property and Standing: Anti-Abolitionist Mobs in Jacksonian America* (New York: Oxford University Press, 1970), 129–130.

9. Adapted from W. J. Rorabaugh, *The Alcoholic Republic: An American Tradition* (New York: Oxford University Press, 1979), 173–175.

10. Laurel Thatcher Ulrich, *A Midwife's Tale: The Life of Martha Ballard, Based on Her Diary, 1785–1812* (New York: Alfred A. Knopf, 1990), 182–183.

11. Gerda Lerner, *The Grimké Sisters from South Carolina* (New York: Schocken, 1971), 99.

12. Thomas E. Jeffrey, *State Parties and National Politics, North Carolina, 1815–1861* (Athens, Ga.: University of Georgia Press, 1989), p. 49.

13. Robert P. Sutton, *Revolution to Secession: Constitution Making in the Old Dominion* (Charlottesville, Va.: University of Virginia Press, 1989), p. 52.

14. Edward H. Carr, *What Is History?* (New York: Vintage Books, 1962), pp. 32–33.

# 7 NARRATIVE: TELLING THE STORY

## *The Way West*

The most popular and compelling historical writing is narrative: the *re*telling of a story. The secret of historical narration is to capture change over time — narrative answers the question, What happened next? Historical narrative focuses on the fortunes and misfortunes of people, merging their many stories into a whole. The narrator selects the most striking and representative details, keeping the story flowing and the reader's attention fixed. Because of its subject matter — human action — narrative can be both swift and deep. Good narrative carries us away with its drive and yet allows us to identify with individuals' hopes and fears.

Narration can be difficult. According to historian Bernard Bailyn, historians must be "narrators of worlds in motion — worlds as complex, unpredictable, and transient, as our own. The historian must re-tell, with a new richness, the story of . . . the worlds of the past."[1] Recently Bailyn has joined other leading historians in a general call for more and better historical narratives.

One of the most popular subjects in American history, westward migration, lends itself to narrative. Continually thrust together in encounters neither side really planned, with consequences no one fully understood, Native Americans and Euro-Americans remade the face of the West. Signs of heroism, cowardice, and tragedy marked every trail to Oregon, California, and Texas. Chapter 7 reviews the basic skills of narration and then offers you the opportunity to transform a collection of excerpts from primary and secondary sources into a short narrative of people and places on the way west.

## The Parts of a Narrative

The most striking characteristic of well-written narrative is its ability to carry a reader along from beginning to end. The best narrators seem to have taken to heart the advice that the king gave to the white rabbit at the trial of the knave of hearts in *Alice in Wonderland:* "Begin at the beginning," the king said, very gravely, "and go on till you come to the end. Then stop."

The beginning of a story sets the scene; it whets your appetite for what is to come. Instead of merely summarizing the rest of the story, a good beginning gives you a taste of the plot, propounds a problem, sets a scene, or introduces you to a key character. The best beginnings grab your attention; you want to read more.

Good endings satisfy you; they convince you that what you have read was well worth the effort. In historical narrative, a good ending not only brings the story to a close, but reassures you that you have learned something. A good ending is also suspenseful; it should leave you reaching for the telephone, wishing you could call the author and ask for more.

The middle of the story should not just be the link between beginning and end. A good middle envelops you, drawing you into the tale. From the best historical writers you expect a new twist, an exciting episode, a sparkling insight, or a moving characterization on every page.

## EXERCISE 1: *Beginning, Middle, and End*

The following three passages are taken from historian Paul Horgan's prize-winning *Great River: The Rio Grande in North American History.* Horgan was a superb stylist and a riveting storyteller. The first passage comes from the beginning of his book; the next from the middle, and the last from near the end. Read them and think about why Horgan put them where he did. Also note his use of illustrative detail. Then answer the questions that follow.

**A** Horgan begins with this description of the sources of the Rio Grande:

> The mountain system of the northern Rio Grande was a vast secret world. Wandering Indians there made shrines of twig and feather and bone, and went their ways. Close to the high clouds that made their rivers, inhuman peaks doubled the roar of thunder, or hissed with sheets of rain, or abided in massive silence. Below them lay every variation of park and meadow and lost lake; gashed canyon and rocky roomlike . . . temples of the high wilderness.[2]

1. How does Horgan's choice of opening fit the subject of his book — the river

   itself? _____

   _____

2. Does his dramatic depiction of the mountain vastness whet your appetite for

   more of his story? If so, why? _____

   _____

**B** On the banks of the Rio Grande many peoples found homes, hunted, and made war on each other. Among these the Comanche were much respected and feared. They ride through the middle of Horgan's book, cynical and hardened, pursuing the vanishing buffalo:

> Superbly mounted, [the Comanche] used cured sheepskins or pieces of buffalo hides to ride on, and their bridles were made of rawhide. They were armed with bows made of [hardwood], metal-tipped arrows, ash-wood lances, shields of buffalo hide edged with turkey feathers, a flint-stone battle axe, and sometimes with rifles, bowie knives, and machetes. . . . In Camp their tepees rose and fell as if by magic — the women were expert at handling the long poles and skins with which the shelters were made. The tepee seemed like a great garment, as it were, drawn about the shoulders of a seated Indian giant.[3]

**FIGURE 7.1** *George Catlin,* Comanche Village in Texas *(1834)*

1. How does Horgan's account of the Comanche's ways capture your imagination?

   _____

   _____

2. In particular, how does the variety of their weaponry suggest that they belong in the middle of the story? _____

   _____

3. How does Horgan's account foreshadow the life-and-death struggle between the Comanche and the Texans that he would soon describe? _____

   _____

   **C** The end of Horgan's story is poignant. The frontier West gave way to the benefits and costs of settlement. Gone were the vast herds of buffalo and their natural predators:

   > On barbed-wire fences, like symbols of the new order of affairs over the controlled range lands, dead, skinned coyotes were impaled in a frieze — twenty or thirty of them at a time. They were stretched in mid-air with a lean, racing look of unearthly nimbleness, running nowhere; and their skulled teeth had the smile of their own ghosts, wits of the plains. . . . The day of unrestrained predators was over.[4]

1. How does this passage make you feel about the end of the frontier? _____

   _____

2. What images in particular capture a mood of something passing into memory?

_____

_____

3. How does the imagery fit into the ending of the story? _____

_____

# Making Your Point

Narrative must be convincing. Every twist and turn in the narrative should persuade a reader to believe the author's reconstruction of events. Narrative is argument, and argument rests on an author's choice of details and arrangement of facts, a series of decisions about what to include and what to omit. Every sentence in a narrative could be made longer by the insertion of more information or cut short. Every paragraph could be extended or pruned in the same way. You have to judge what kinds of information belong together.

### EXERCISE 2: *Unnecessary Information in Narrative Paragraphs*

In each of the following three passages there is a sentence that should be removed because it is not essential to the narrative or contradicts the other sentences. Underline the sentence that can be omitted. Be prepared to defend your choice.

1. Americans yearned for a literature of their own. They wanted to take their place with other "refined" European countries as a producer of literature and art. Much effort went into the search for an author to rival Sir Walter Scott in popularity. For a time James Fenimore Cooper seemed to fill the bill. His novelistic accounts of the frontier became best sellers. Rampant racism undermined all these literary efforts. Cooper's portrait of the countryside was unrealistic, but catered to Americans' romantic notions of heroic frontiersmen and damsels in distress.

2. Southerners like Robert E. Lee and Jefferson Davis began their careers in the military during the Mexican American war of 1845. In the course of the war, they came to believe that a martial spirit, dash, heroism, and persistence were the keys to victory. The old smooth-bore muskets were rapidly replaced by rifles, giving the soldiers far greater range and accuracy. Lee and Davis were to stress these virtues when they went to war again, this time to defend the confederacy against federal forces. The result was a theory of war based upon attack rather than defense and at Gettysburg the needless sacrifice of thousands of confederate men and boys.

3. As eager as they were to transform wild nature into a landscape of farms and towns, Americans clung to a vision of wilderness as a repository of virtue. They professed their love of undisturbed nature even as they transformed the forests and the prairies into fields and factories. When they depicted railroads belching smoke and flaming coals in valleys that were once quiet and green, they framed the picture with the symbols of untamed nature — rolling wooded hills, bubbling streams, and undisturbed wildlife. There was no limit to some Americans' enthusiasm when it came to reforming their countrymen's bad habits.

## EXERCISE 3: *Inference from Narrative*

The sequence of argument in a narrative must be logical, and the reader must be able to follow that logic. Every arrangement of facts into arguments requires readers to make logical jumps. Read the following. After each passage you will find four statements. Can they be inferred from the narrative in the passage? If a statement is a logical inference from the narrative, write *true* in the space provided. If a statement is contradicted by the author's account, write *false*. If there is insufficient evidence one way or the other, write *cannot determine.*

A. If many [nineteenth-century European immigrants to the west] at first intended to emulate the [earliest] backwoodsmen . . . whose thrilling exploits they had read in American works of fiction, the resolve generally faded . . . upon learning that the backwoods lay far from the port . . . [where they landed]. Those who nevertheless pursued their original intention soon regretted their [boldness]. The boundless forest was a disheartening sight, and the American ax a dangerous instrument in the hands of a novice. After the first tree was felled with painful toil, the forest still loomed dense and gloomy; and the knowledge of all the labor that must be expended to clear each acre for corn . . . deepened the feeling of discouragement. The experience was one they shared with the colonists of two centuries before . . . [for among the first backwoodsmen] every third blow of the ax was drowned out by an oath.[5]

1. Nineteenth-century immigrants to America were unfamiliar with the experiences of their predecessors. _____

2. The nineteenth-century immigrants were not used to seeing so many trees.

   _____

3. The lesson the nineteenth-century immigrants learned from the forest was to return to towns and cities. _____

4. In their initial experience with the American wilderness, there was little difference between the nineteenth-century immigrants and the backwoodsmen who preceded them. _____

B. Women aged more noticeably on the frontier than did men. Because of constant childbearing and the immensely difficult job of maintaining a home, caring for the children, and working in the fields, a thirty-year-old woman was already old and worn out . . . Because women were at a premium, however [there were so few], they obtained certain advantages not granted their sisters in settled areas. . . . It was Wyoming Territory and Colorado that [first] granted women the vote . . . In order to attract women to the new frontiers, Western territories granted wives the right to hold their land separately from their husbands. In the 1850s, single women in Oregon were given 320 acres if they would migrate there.[6]

1. There were relatively few women in frontier areas. _____

2. Women on the frontier were weaker than frontiersmen. _____

3. Frontierswomen did not stay on the frontier long. _____

4. Without women, life on the frontier would have been far harsher for men.

   _____

## EXERCISE 4: *Using Sources*

The time has come for you to craft your own story. We will give you the pieces; you must weave them into a narrative. You choose where to begin and where to end, and how to arrange and embellish your arguments.

The following map, illustrations, and reading selections include primary and secondary sources. Examine each selection. After each, answer the study questions and follow the instructions.

**A** The emigrants who went west before the Civil War did not have good maps of the terrain they were to cross. They hired guides, sometimes sought the aid of passing Indians, and followed natural landmarks on their way west. The map in Figure 7.2 was drawn for a modern textbook and therefore contains more information than was available to many of the pioneers.

1. What were the major trails west? _____

_____

2. Where did they go? _____

_____

3. What obstacles lay between the jumping-off sites and the Pacific shore? _____

_____

4. How many miles separated Nauvoo from Salt Lake City? Independence from Astoria? _____

_____

**B** The grassy plains were the home of many Indian tribes. The Arapaho, Comanche, Cheyenne, Lakota (Sioux), Blackfoot, Crow, Snake (Shoshone), and Pawnee had all mastered the horse and vied for control of vast stretches of prairie. Although all the tribes hunted and fished, their main source of sustenance was the vast herds of buffalo that roamed the grasslands. The Indians used every part of the buffalo, eating the meat, wearing the hides, drinking from the hollowed-out horns, and making bowstrings from the sinews and arrowheads and fishing hooks from the bones. In 1837 a twenty-seven-year-old Baltimore artist named Jacob Alfred Miller traveled through the high plains, stopping to make drawings of the Indians. Figure 7.3 shows his later painting of a buffalo hunt.

1. From the painting, what can you deduce about the Indians' skill with their horses? _____

_____

2. What was their attitude toward the hunt? _____

_____

**C** Midway through his journey Miller stopped to paint the portrait of a Snake Indian chief, Ma-Wo-Ma (Little Chief). Little Chief, a sturdy six-footer, gave Miller a present of a drawing that the chief had made on a buffalo hide. The exchange of presents was a vital social courtesy among Plains Indians. The drawing (Figure 7.4) strikingly portrays the self-image of a mighty warrior.

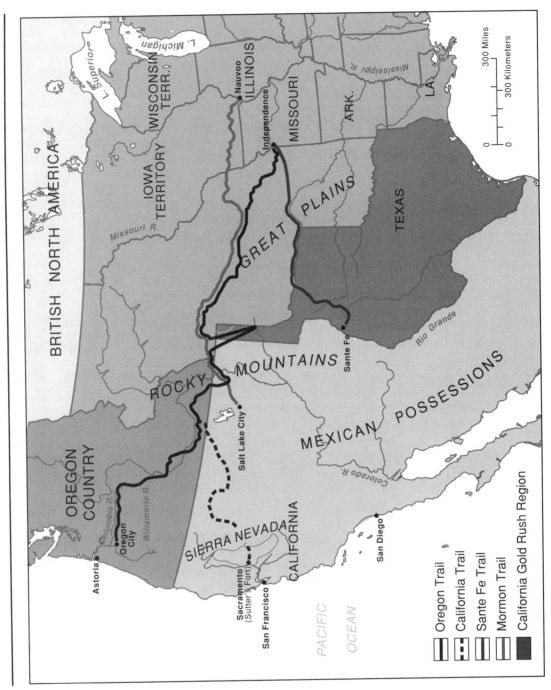

**FIGURE 7.2** *Westward Migration Routes, 1850*

**FIGURE 7.4** *Buffalo-Hide Drawing: Ma-Wo-Ma (Little Chief) (1837)*

FIGURE 7.5 *John Gast,* **American Progress** *(1872)*

1. Where is Ma-Wo-Ma in the picture? _____

_____

2. What is he doing, and to whom? _____

_____

3. What weapons did the Indians use? _____

_____

4. What do you suppose the fifteen arrows represent? _____

_____

   **D** Indian artists had no monopoly on symbolic depiction or heroic virtues. The illustration in Figure 7.5 is a painting entitled *American Progress.* Its central figure is Liberty, carrying aloft a symbol of progress, the telegraph lines. She flies above the plains, westward, the Rocky Mountains in front of her and civilization (cities, railroads, farms) behind. The buffalo, the Indians, and the wild animals flee before her.

1. What is the artist's attitude toward the Indians? _____

_____

2. How are the Indians portrayed? _____

_____

3. What occupations are represented among the Euro-Americans at the bottom of the painting? _____

_____

4. What does the artist suggest will be the outcome of the migration of these men and women? _____

_____

5. How might this assumption about progress enter into Euro-American–Native American encounters? _____

_____

**E** Before the settlers began to cross the plains and mountains of the American West in great numbers, there came the trappers, explorers, and soldiers. One of the last of these expeditions was led by a bold and ambitious army officer named John C. Frémont. With him rode a bad-tempered and sharp-eyed German engineer and mapmaker, Charles Preuss. The selections below from Preuss's diary of the second expedition to California in 1843 and 1844 give you an idea of how chancy the mountain crossings could be:

*December 1*
*[1843]*

Here I am in the mountains, sitting on an old fir trunk, with thin snow around me and a mule beside me, waiting for the caravan. I had to give up my place in the wagon. Frémont said that progress was too slow on the bad roads and gave the wagon away. Yet the cannon causes just as much delay, and unless he presents it to someone as he did the wagon, we shall move ahead slowly. . . .

God only knows what we shall still have to go through on this winter journey. We still have two thousand miles back to the States. . . . Yesterday we made only eight miles, and today it will not be more than five. . . . Our Indian guides gave us to understand that we shall find no grass for two days. Unless that is a lie, I don't see how we can get our wretched animals through. We ourselves are now well provided. Flour, peas, sugar, and coffee were purchased in large quantities at Vancouver. The beef cattle follow the caravan; one was slaughtered and the meat divided for several mules to carry. This California beef is very savory and almost as good as buffalo. Whenever our cook has time to fix a stewed steak in the iron pot, we lead the life of a lord. . . .

*December 3*

Tonight we are without water and are camping on a slope where the sun has left some snow. I have eaten so much salty food and this tobacco makes one's mouth so dry that I cannot melt enough snow to drink. . . .

*January 5, 1844*

We've been sitting here for three days, wrapped in fog, on a miserable plateau surrounded by bare hills. The animals are dying, one after the other. Very little grass, snow instead of water. We have turned more to the southwest. We shall probably cross over to California. It appears to be impossible to move with such animals through the plains in winter, almost without grass and water. What a Christmas and New Year we have had this year!

*[February 3]*

We are getting deeper and deeper into mountains and snow. We pay one roving Indian after the other to guide us across. . . .

The snow is terribly deep, and we can make only a few miles each day. I am almost barefoot. This surpasses every discomfort that I have experienced so far. With the old Prussian surveying office [where Preuss had worked] one often had bad days, but one could expect comfortable quarters in the evening. Here a buffalo hide is spread on the snow — that is the feather bed. . . .

*February 24*

Finally we are out of the snow. Yesterday was still a bad day: snow, rocks, brush. Terrible march. In nine hours we made three miles, until we came to a place where another fork joins the river. . . . The sun had melted almost all the snow. It was quite steep where we had to go up and down across canyons; in general, however, there was earthy soil under the fir trees, etc.; mighty boulders thrown in between. We made about twelve miles in four hours and found some grass and horsetail for our hungry beasts. We therefore made a halt, for such spots are rather scarce here in the forest.

Another horse was just shot; I hope the eating of horse meat will soon be over. Tomorrow, I think, we should come pretty close to the valley. Then my Polly [Preuss's horse] can recuperate with good grass so that I can ride again, for walking is, after all, a little hard. Horse meat gives no strength, and every student of nature knows that peas contain little nourishment.

The mules grew so hungry that they ate the tail of Fitzpatrick's horse, also parts of saddles, my bridle, etc.[7]

Underline the most striking details in the passage.

1. What features of the land most impressed Preuss? _____

   _____

2. What hardships most annoyed or frightened him? _____

   _____

**F** While Preuss and Frémont descended into the Sacramento Valley of California, a young Bostonian named Francis Parkman was setting out on his own journey to Oregon. He had little respect for the migrants, who trekked across the great plains in search of new homes. Parkman was there for the adventure, an adventure he later described in his book *The Oregon Trail*. The portion from it reproduced below was originally written at the end of May, 1846.

*May 28th.* Wolves all night. Camped on Little Blue [River]. Saw wolves and two antelopes in the morning. Grave of a child 4 yrs. old — May 1845.

Henry hunted in vain for antelopes. Nooned [spent midday] on Little Blue. Made a very long afternoon march — hour after hour over a perfect level — not very well. Sorel wounded an antelope. After twelve miles riding, approached Little Blue again. Immense masses of blue, lurid clouds in the west shadowed the green prairie, and the sun glared through purple and crimson. As we draw near the valley of the stream, a furious wind, presaging a storm, struck us. We galloped down in the face of it — horses snorting with fear. Rode to the ground — up went the tent and on came the storm.

*May 29ᵗʰ*. Left camp — saw plenty of antelopes and fired at one across the river. Kept along the Little Blue, and just before nooning had great trouble in crossing a tributary creek [Pawnee Creek?]. As we (we) were dining, Henry brought in a fine antelope — a very welcome acquisition as our bacon is almost gone. Afternoon — more antelope and turkeys. Scenery very beautiful and prairielike. The Capt. very merry, riding off in all directions and running a wolf over the prairie. Bones of game scattered in all directions, indicating a surround. Moved rapidly and merrily — camped on a beautiful plain, hard by the woods that fringe the Little Blue. Flowers — prairie peas — *pommes blanches*.

Mounted guard for the first time last night — three hours. Middle watch to me and Delorier tonight. Delorier is a true Canadian — all his acts and thoughts are subject to the will of his *bourgeois* [boss].

Met yesterday in a rough meadow by the Little Blue [River] two Delaware Inds. returning from a hunt — one of them a remarkably handsome fellow.

*May 30ᵗʰ*. Made a very hard day's work — came more than thirty miles from the Blue [River] to the Platte [River]. We had all along mistaken our route, thinking that we were less advanced than in fact we were. Soon after leaving the Blue, saw two men, Turner and another, come back from the emigrants [settlers on their way to Oregon or California] in search of an ox. They set us right, telling us we were 26 miles from the river. Just before seeing us, they had met six Pawnees, who wanted to change horses, and laid hand on the bridle of one of them, till threatened with a pistol — the only weapon they had. . . . Camped late — an emigrant came to us, on his way to look for Turner — he told us that Robinson's party were encamped three miles off — that the four waggons that had joined us, and got ahead a few days ago, were in advance — and that a large hunting-party of Pawnees were encamped close to them.

This afternoon, passed a very large Pawnee trail, and a small foot trail recently travelled.

*May 31ˢᵗ*. Early this morning, the Pawnees, about 30 in number, passed a short distance from our camp — a hunting-party — no women, these being probably planting corn at the village. Rather mean-looking fellows, each with a bow and arrows — led horses, loaded with dry meat. The chief walked behind — I gave him a piece of tobacco, which very much pleased him. . . .

Papin reports that the Mormons are a few miles ahead — that the Pawnees have taken 10 of their horses, and whipped one of their men into camp — that the Sioux have been out in force, and driven off the buffalo — all this alarms the Capt. exceedingly.[8]

Underline the most striking details in Parkman's diary.

1. What did he think of the Pawnee? _____

_____

2. What impression did he have of the scenery? _____

_____

3. What did he expect to happen when the settlers and the Indians got too close

to one another? _____

_____

**G** Women also set out on the way west. Though they walked alongside husbands, fathers, and sons, their story was different from their menfolk's, as John Mack Faragher and Christine Stansell remind you.

> The disintegration of the physical base of domesticity [furniture was the first thing dumped when the wagons were too heavy to cross a river] was symptomatic of an even more serious disruption in the female subculture. Because the wagon trains so often broke into smaller units, many women were stranded in parties without other women. Since there were usually two or more men in the same family party, some male friendships and bonds remained intact for the duration of the journey. But by midway in the trip, female companionship, so valued by nineteenth-century women, was unavailable to the solitary wife in a party of hired men, husband, and children that had broken away from a larger train. Emergencies and quarrels, usually between men, broke up the parties. . . . On the day [one family] separated from the others, [a woman] wrote in her journal: "The women came over to bid me goodbye, for we were to go alone, all alone. They said there was no color in my face. I felt as if there was none." She perceived the separation as a banishment, almost a death sentence: "There is something peculiar in such a parting on the Plains, one there realizes what a goodbye is." . . . Uprootedness took its toll in debilitation and numbness. After a hard week, men "lolled around in the tents and on their blankets seeming to realize that the 'Sabbath was made for man,' " resting on the palpable achievements of miles covered and rivers crossed. In contrast, the women "could not fully appreciate physical rest, and were rendered more uneasy by the continual passing of emigrant trains all day long. . . . To me, much of the day was spent in meditating over the past and in forebodings for the future."
>
> The ultimate expression of this alienation was the pressure to turn back, to retrace steps to the old life. Occasionally anxiety or bewilderment erupted into open revolt against going on.
>
> *This morning our company moved on, except one family. The woman got mad and wouldn't budge or let the children go. He had the cattle hitched on for three hours and coaxed her to go, but she wouldn't stir.*
>
> Short of violent resistance, it was always possible that circumstances would force a family to reconsider and turn back. During a cholera scare in 1852, "women cried, begging their men to take them back." When the men reluctantly relented, the writer observed that "they did the hooking up of their oxen in a spiritless sort of way," while "some of the girls and women were laughing." There was little lost and much regained for women in a decision to abandon the migration.
>
> Both sexes worked, and both sexes suffered. Yet women lacked a sense of inclusion and a cultural rationale to give meaning to the suffering and the work; no augmented sense of self or role emerged from augmented privation. Both women and men also complained, but women expanded their caviling to a generalized critique of the whole enterprise. Margaret Chambers felt "as if we had left all civilization behind us" after crossing the Missouri, . . . Civilization was far more to these women than law, books, and municipal governments; it was pianos, church societies, daguerreotypes, mirrors — in short, their homes. At their most hopeful, the exiles perceived the Trail as a hellish but necessary transition to a land where they could renew their domestic mission: "Each advanced step of the slow, plodding cattle carried us farther and farther from civilization into a desolate, barbarous country. . . . But our new home lay beyond all this and was a shining beacon that beckoned us on, inspiring our hearts with hope and courage."[9]

Underline the most striking details in the passage.

1. What was it like for women traveling west, according to this selection? _____

2. What did women resent most about life on the trail? _____

_____

3. What evidence does the passage offer for this resentment? _____

_____

**(H)** Some migrants lost their fortunes, their children, their parents, and finally their own lives as they trekked across the continent. The most infamous of these tragedies involved the "Donner party" of emigrants from Illinois. At their head were two patriarchs, George and Jacob Donner. With them came their families, their friends, and their servants. Half of them died of hunger in the high passes of the Sierra Nevada, the gateway to California. Their fate has become a symbol of the hardships of the trail, for, trapped in the snow, they resorted to cannibalism.

> There is no point in devoting to the Donner party the space it receives in this book except as it provides one of the varieties of frontier experience. It has been a favorite story of historians and novelists because it is concentrated, because the horror composes a drama. But the reader of this book will understand that the disaster which overtook the Donner party was part of the trail's *if*, one factor in the equation of chance under which emigration across the mountains and desert traveled. The fate of the Donners or its equivalent was, as a hazard, part of the equipment packed in every white-top [covered wagon] that pulled up the slope beyond Fort Laramie, this year, the years before it, and for some years still to come. Whether the risk was to be taken successfully or unsuccessfully depended on chance, weather, skill, intelligence, and character — all inscrutable. . . . The Donners were not the only emigrants who disintegrated in panic, and the fact which the public chiefly remembers about them, their cannibalism, was no novelty in the West. It had occurred along the route they traveled, and when, in the last days of 1848, Frémont's fourth expedition stalled in the San Juan snows, Bill Williams' detachment probably killed and certainly ate one of their companions. Kit Carson remarked of Bill Williams that in starving times no man should walk ahead of him on the trail, and old Bill shared that reputation with numerous others. In fact, the last resource of starving men is a commonplace.
>
> It is as the commonplace or typical just distorted that the Donners must be seen. Beyond Fort Laramie every stretch of the trail they traveled, at some time during the history of emigration, saw one or another party just escaping disaster, and a number of stretches saw some parties not altogether escaping it.[10]

Underline the most striking details in the passage.

1. What is the author's main message? _____

_____

2. Was the Donner party's fate unusual? _____

_____

**(I)** One member of the Donner party, Patrick Breen, left a diary, and a portion of it serves as the last selection for your narrative writing assignment.

*Friday, Nov. 20th 1846* came to this place on the 31st of last month that it snowed we went on to the pass the snow so deep we were unable to find the road, when within 3 miles of the summit then turned back to this shanty on the Lake, [Charles T.] Stanton came one day after we arrived here we again took our teams & waggons & made another unsuccessful attempt to cross in company with Stanton we returned to the shanty it continuing to snow all the time we were here we now have Killed most part of our cattle having to stay here untill next Spring & live on poor beef without bread or salt[.] It snowed during the space of eight days with little intermission, after our arrival here, the remainder of time up to this day was clear & pleasant frezing at night the snow nearly gone from the valleys.

*Sat 21st* fine morning wind N.W. 22 of our company are about Starting across the mountain this morning including Stanton & his indians, some clouds flying thawed today wind E

*Sunday 22nd* froze hard last night this a fine clear morning, wind E. S. E. no account from those on the mountains

*Monday 23rd* same weather wind W the Expedition across the mountains returned after an unsucesful attempt . . .

*Thursday the 26th* began to snow yesterday in the evening now rains or sleet the mountaniers dont start today the wind about W, wet & muddy

*Friday 27* Continues to snow, the ground not covered, wind W dull prospect for crossing the Mountains . . .

*December 1st Tuesday* Still Snowing wind W snow about 5½ feet or 6 deep difficult to get wood. no going from the house Completely housed up looks as likely for snow as when it Commenced, our cattle all Killed but three or four of them, the horses & Stantons mules gone & Cattle suppose lost in the Snow no hopes of finding them alive . . .

*Frid. 5th [January]* snowd. hard all untill 12 O'clock at night wind still continues to blow hard from the S. W. to day pretty clear a few clouds only Peggy very uneasy for fear we shall all perrish with hunger we have but alittle meat left & only part of 3 hides has to support Mrs. Reid, she has nothing left but one hide & it is on Graves shanty Milt. is livi[n]g there & likely will Keep that hide [William M.] Eddys child [Margaret] died last night-

*Satd. 6th* it snowd. faster last night & to day than it has done this winter & still Continues without an intermission wind S. W. Murphys folks or Keyburgs say they cant eat hides. I wish we had enough of them Mrs [Eleanor] Eddy very weak.

*Sund. 7th* Ceasd. to snow last after one of the most Severe Storms we Experienced this winter the snow fell about 4 feet deep I had to shovel the snow off our shanty this morning it thaw so fast & thawd. during the whole storm to day it is quite pleasant wind S. W. Milt here today says Mrs. Reid has to get ahide from M.rs Murphy & McCutchins [William McCutchen's] child [Harriet] died 2nd of this Month

*Mond 8th* fine clear morning wind S. W. froze hard last [night] Spitzer died last night about 3 Oclock to [day?] we will bury him in the snow Mrs Eddy died on the night of the 7th [*deleted*: Mrs Murp]

*Tuesd. 9th* Mrs Murphy here this morning [William M.] pikes child [Catherine] all but dead Milt at Murphys not able to get out of bed Keyburg never gets up says he is not able. John went down to day to bury Mrs Eddy & child heard nothing from Graves for 2 or 3 days Mrs Murphy just now going to Graves fine moing wind S. E. froze hard last night begins to thaw in the Sun

*Wednd. 10th* beautiful morning Wind W. froze hard last night, to day thawing in the Sun Milt Elliot died las night at Murphys Shanty about 9 Oclock P.M. Mrs Reid went there this morning to see after his effects. J Denton trying to borrow meat for Graves had none to give they have nothing but hides all are entirely out of meat but a little we have our hides are nearly all eat up but with Gods help spring will soon smile upon us . . .[11]

Underline the most striking details in the passage.

1. What happened to the Donner party as they reached the high mountain passes?

_____

_____

2. What was their decision in response to this unexpected occurrence? _____

_____

3. What then happened to the emigrants? _____

_____

4. How did they cope with the winter in the mountains? _____

_____

## EXERCISE 5: *Telling Your Story: The Way West*

Using the primary and secondary sources from exercise 4, write a historical essay of four to five pages (third person, please, using the past tense) describing what it was like on the way west before the Civil War. Begin the task by reviewing the readings and illustrations, including your own short answers and the parts you underlined. Write your main ideas below:

_____

_____

_____

_____

Next, on a separate sheet of paper write an outline that lists your main ideas and the supporting evidence you will use. From your outline, write your first draft, including appropriate citations. Be sure your beginning grabs the reader's interest, your middle is detailed and lively, and your ending provides a satisfying conclusion. Ask yourself whether your ideas flow logically from paragraph to paragraph. Is your style colorful? Does each main point you make have sufficient support? Have you incorporated interesting excerpts from the primary sources? Your choice of a story line makes the narrative your own. Do not be afraid to reach your own conclusions. Originality is an important part of every narrative. Ask a friend to read your draft. Did he or she enjoy it?

Write a second draft to correct any inaccuracies and supply any omissions. Proofread your second draft for spelling, punctuation, and grammar. Prepare and submit your final draft.

As you examined the selections above, you might have asked yourself: how typical were the experiences of these people? The Donner party's fate was gruesome, but how likely were settlers to find themselves caught in the high mountain passes late in the season? What was the average migrant like? How did the pioneers' experiences vary over the course of time and from place to place? By asking questions like these, you shift your focus from the particular to the general, from individual experience to the common experience, and from narrative to analysis. Chapter 8 will help you to gain these skills.

## NOTES

1. Bernard Bailyn, "The Challenge of Modern Historiography," *American Historical Review* 87 (1982): 24.
2. Paul Horgan, *Great River: The Rio Grande in North American History* (New York: Funk and Wagnalls, 1968), 2:460.
3. Ibid., 2:850.
4. Ibid., 2:886.
5. Marcus Lee Hansen, *The Immigrant in American History* [1940] (New York, Harper & Row, 1964), 66.
6. June Sochen, *Herstory: A Woman's View of American History* (New York: Alfred Publishing, 1974), 114.
7. Charles Preuss, *Exploring with Frémont,* tr. and ed. Erwin G. and Elizabeth Gudde (Norman, Okla.: University of Oklahoma Press, 1958), 99–113.
8. Mason Wade, ed., *The Journals of Francis Parkman* (New York: Harper & Row, 1947), 430–433.
9. Johnny Mack Faragher and Christine Stansell, "Women and Their Families on the Overland Trail to California and Oregon, 1842–1847," *Feminist Studies* 2 (1975), 150–166.
10. Bernard De Voto, *The Year of Decision: 1846* (Boston: Houghton Mifflin, 1943), 340–341.
11. "The Breen Diary" in Dale Morgan, ed., *Overland in 1846: Diaries and Letters of the California-Oregon Trail* (Georgetown, Calif.: The Talisman Press, 1963), 306–322.

# 8 ANALYSIS: GROUPS, NUMBERS, AND PATTERNS IN HISTORY

## *The Antebellum South*

When you write a narrative, you tell a story. You need not decide if your story is typical, nor try to compare the subject of your story to other subjects. You are free to ignore questions about larger trends in the past. If all historical writing were narrative in style, however, history would be a very narrow discipline. It would exclude analysis of groups, numbers, and patterns.

In ordinary speech we define analysis as the breaking apart of a whole to examine its parts. Analysis is the opposite of synthesis, the assembly of the many parts into a whole. Historians must do both analysis and synthesis to understand and explain what happened in the past. Historical analysis does not supplant or preclude narration but rather overlaps it.

Another way to capture the difference that exists between an analytical approach to history and a narrative approach is to think of analytical historians as "lumpers" and narrative historians as "splitters." The analytical historians "lump" together similar events, people, and objects into groups and use numerical methods to find patterns. They seek to uncover and explain the continuities, trends, comparisons, and connections in history. By contrast, narrative historians regard the discrete, momentary, distinct, and distinctive in the past as the most important characteristic of any study of history. They produce richly textured accounts of particular people or events, in effect "splitting" history into its many fragments and focusing on them one at a time.

## History and the Social Sciences

Analytical writing about history is very popular among scholars today. In part this has resulted from the emergence of social history. Social history requires a keen appreciation of the role of groups in society, and social historians often use numerical methods to explain the dynamics of group formation and behavior. Social history also emphasizes long-term shifts in the shape and conduct of these groups.

Analytical historical interpretations, including social history, would be impossible without the rise of the social sciences of sociology, economics, and cultural anthropology at the end of the nineteenth and the beginning of the twentieth centuries. Analytical historians are always borrowing concepts and methods from the social sciences. Although narrative historians ordinarily confine themselves to the language and ideas of the people they study — indeed, sometimes these historians' writings begin to resemble the prose style of their subjects — analytical historians mimic vogues in economic research, sociological concepts, and anthropological findings. Returning to the question in Chapter 6 of whether history was an art or a science, narrative historical writers would choose the former option, analytical historical writers the latter.

## Groups

Narrative focuses on the uniqueness of particular people and events; analysis requires you to think about similarities and connections among groups of people — for example, families, neighborhoods, communities, and voluntary associations — and groups of things — for example, prices, wages, import and export figures. You cannot find continuities or make comparisons unless you conceptualize history as group activity over time.

To frame analytical questions about how and why groups acted as they did, you must begin to think in terms of the characteristics that define a group. Certain characteristics are obvious to the observer. Other features are not so visible. They have to be found through research.

### EXERCISE 1: *What Makes a Group?*

This exercise introduces the technique of grouping. Look around the classroom. The people in it can be sorted into different groups in a number of ways. In what four ways might you categorize your classmates?

1. _____

2. _____

3. _____

4. _____

Each of these four ways of sorting your class is based on a categorization that you formulated. Each of these categories divides one large group — your class — into smaller groups. Each smaller group is united by one or more salient characteristics. You may have used observable physical variables, like height, age, or gender to arrange your groups, or selected groups on the basis of observed behavior — habits of dress, attentiveness in class, or personality traits. You may have recalled your classmates' participation in an event (for example, the grades they got on the last exam) to group them. To isolate and examine groups, historians employ categories based on social and economic status, age and other population criteria; categories derived from time and place, and distinctions growing out of the behavior of their subjects.

### EXERCISE 2: *Studying Nearby Groups*

You are surrounded by groups and no doubt belong to some of them. The United States is a nation of joiners. The groups you belong to are not mutually exclusive. They overlap one another, sometimes in harmony, sometimes in competition for your time and loyalty. One group we all belong to is our neighborhood. A neighborhood is both a group of people living in close proximity to each other and a group of dwellings. David E. Kyvig and Myron A. Marty have prepared a series of questions about neighborhoods for students in their *Nearby History: Exploring the Past Around You* (1982). These questions help you to turn something with which you are already familiar into a subject for historical study. Think about the neighborhood in which you were reared, or, alternatively, the one in which you now reside, and try to answer the following questions about it.

1. What are the boundaries of your neighborhood? How are they defined? What distinguishes your neighborhood from those around it? _____

    _____

    _____

2. What is the central social focus of your neighborhood? Where do the people in it congregate? _____

    _____

    _____

3. How and why has the size and shape of your neighborhood changed over the years? What buildings or open spaces appeared or disappeared during this time that changed the neighborhood? _____

    _____

    _____

4. How did people in the neighborhood travel to work? What kinds of workplaces were there in the neighborhood? How have these changed over the years?

    _____

    _____

    _____

5. Who lived in the neighborhood? What family ties, religious ties, or ethnic ties predominated among these people? Have these characteristics changed? If so, how? _____

    _____

    _____

6. How does the neighborhood fit into the larger community (city, county, or other larger place)? What historical events brought people in the neighborhood together? What events caused them to divide among themselves? _____

    _____

    _____

By considering these questions you have begun the analytical history of your neighborhood. Although you are telling its story, you cannot tell the story without focusing on groups and measuring changes in them.

**EXERCISE 3:** *Identifying Groups in Historical Writing*

Often, a historical account that appears to be purely narrative actually deals with groups, and analytical historians often use the writing of narrative historians to select appropriate groups for study. For this exercise, read the two passages following and underline the groups that the author discusses. Remember, a group can be a collection of persons or of things. We have underlined the first group in each passage to help you get started.

A. Demographic mobility was so much a part of life in the slaveholding South that those who yearned for stability were often frustrated. Complaints were most common among the wives of slaveholders who missed the society they left. "I feel almost friendless," a Tennessee mistress wrote to her Virginia friend. "The intimacy of dear and loved relatives have been broken by the bitter pill of separation leaving a faint hope of meeting on earth. I feel exceedingly desolate and lonely.". . . It was women who most consistently protested the wandering ways of their slaveholding husbands. They wrote of their loneliness on the frontier, complained of being left alone for long stretches while their spouses searched for lands out west, and objected when the decision to move was announced.[1]

B. [Visitors to free African-American communities on the coastal islands of Georgia and South Carolina during the Civil War] described ties between kin in different immediate families. "The country people" [one visitor observed] "regard their relations more than the city people; they often walk fifteen miles on a Saturday night to see a cousin." [Another visitor] agreed: "Their affection extends to the whole family. If a cousin is in want, they admit the claim [on them]. Other observers of the wartime Sea Islanders noticed binding ties between members of different immediate families.[2]

## *Numbers*

Thinking about historical events in terms of groups of people or things is the first step in writing analytically. The next step is to select precise measures of differences and similarities within and between groups and changes in group characteristics over time. The most precise measures of differences and changes are numerical — in short, the analytical historian must use numbers.

**EXERCISE 4:** *Hidden Counting*

A vociferous critic of analytical writing once complained that only those things that cannot be counted are ever really important. This statement overlooks the fact that every historian — whether engaged in narration or analysis — resorts to hidden counting. The following two passages are filled with hidden quantifiers, words that indicate rates or quantity. Find them and underline them. We have underlined the first two quantifiers in each passage to get you started.

A. Dueling was a vitally important institution in the antebellum South. The practice first appeared in common use in America among revolutionary war officers during the 1770s and quickly spread to the rest of the nation, but it retreated into the South by the early nineteenth century. It flourished in the slave states even though it was both against the law and widely condemned in public. Even in states without antidueling statutes common law prosecution was possible. But Southern prosecutors, unlike their Northern counterparts, rarely enforced laws against dueling. When a possibility of enforcement existed, duelists crossed borders [of states] or even dueled on borders in order to create just enough ambiguity in legal jurisdiction to discourage indictment. Even when duelists did come to trial, Southern juries almost never found them guilty. If dueling laws provided that public officers swear they had never fought duels, Southern legislatures routinely passed special exception laws.[3]

B. Owners [of slaves in the antebellum South] had <u>various</u> methods of providing religious training. <u>Most</u> of them believed it "pernicious and evil" for slaves to preach at their own services or prayer meetings. Nevertheless, some permitted it. The master or overseer usually attended such meetings, as required by law — and the preacher, naturally, was a trusted slave. In a number of southern towns the bondsmen attended their own churches . . . controlled by a governing board of whites and served by a white pastor. . . . In the regions of small slaveholding, whites and blacks commonly belonged to the same churches; on the large plantations only the domestics accompanied their masters to worship. When there were mixed congregations the slaves sat in the galleries, or were grouped together at the rear. Sometimes they attended special services on Sunday afternoons.[4]

## *Quantification*

All historians employ words like *rise*, *fall*, *many*, and *few*. Analytical writers are more open and sophisticated in quantification, however. Quantification is the measurement of trends or characteristics of data through mathematical methods. These methods need not be difficult to understand.

Some types of evidence lend themselves readily to counting. Interval, or quantitative, data is expressed in integers and decimals, and is commonly used for wages, prices, population figures, and the like. The most common statistical measure of interval data is the mean or average. To compute the mean, the historian adds up the numbers and then divides by the number of cases. For example, to calculate the average number of slaves each Georgia slaveholder possessed in 1850, one adds up the number of slaves in the state according to the U.S. census of 1850 and then divides by the number of slaveholders in the state recorded in the same census. An average can be misleading if "outliers" — cases on the extreme high or low end of the distribution of data — are too numerous or too scanty.

Nominal (sometimes called "categorical") data, including racial and ethnic categories or gender, is qualitative and less amenable to statistical manipulation than interval data, but nominal data can be counted. To measure the most important characteristics in a set of nominal data, the historian ascertains the mode. The mode is simply the most common qualitative characteristic of the cases. For example, to answer the question Was the typical slave male or female?, one would count the number of male slaves and compare it to the number of female slaves. The gender with the largest count would be the mode. Modes can be calculated for any collection of nominal data.

**EXERCISE 5:** *Recognizing Types of Data*

The distinction between interval data and nominal data is basic to all quantification. With practice, you will easily recognize the difference. Look around your classroom. Find an example of interval data and an example of nominal data. Next, select any page of your textbook. Identify an example of interval data and an example of nominal data.

## *Displaying Quantification: Tables*

Analytical historians often integrate the results of their quantification into the body of their writing. They do not set off percentages, averages, or other measures of amount in any way. By incorporating numbers into their prose, these historians minimize the disruptive effect that their statistical calculations might have on the flow of their accounts. On other occasions, analytical historians interrupt their accounts with obvious forms of quantitative display, including tables and graphs. These quantitative displays can be compared in impact and function to long block quotations. Both break the flow of the page in order to force the reader to pay attention to the evidence. Behind each such quantitative exhibit is a twofold task — (1) to give a full, clear, and informative presentation of the data, and (2) to spotlight the most important relationships within the data.

Tables summarize and tabulate the characteristics of variables — that which you are counting. Tables are appropriate for both interval and nominal data. They are always comparative; that is, they compare one variable against another or show how a single variable changes over time or place. One variable is displayed across the top or bottom of the table in a row or rows. The second variable is displayed down the table in columns. At the intersection of each column (going up and down) and each row (going from side to side) is an entry. The variation in these entries is what the analytical historian must explain.

## EXERCISE 6: *Reading Tables*

Examine tables A and B. Answer the questions after each of them.

### Table A Cotton Production in the South, 1790–1860

|                  | 1790    | 1820      | 1840      | 1860      |
|------------------|---------|-----------|-----------|-----------|
| Cotton bales     | 4,000   | 73,222    | 1,347,098 | 3,841,416 |
| Number of slaves | 697,897 | 1,538,098 | 2,487,213 | 3,957,760 |

SOURCE: Paul Boyer, et al., *The Enduring Vision, A History of the American People* (Lexington, Mass.: 1990), 1:353.

The two variables are cotton production and the number of slaves.

1. What is the row variable? _____

2. What is the column variable? _____

3. What does the table reveal about changes in the extent of cotton farming in the United States between 1790 and 1860? _____

   _____

4. What about the increase in the number of slaves? _____

   _____

5. Are the two sets of data interval or nominal? _____

6. Do they co-vary (that is, go up and down together)? _____

7. What does your answer to the previous question suggest about the use of slaves in cotton production? _____

   _____

**Table B  Life Expectancy of African-American Women**

| Period | Expectation of Life |
|--------|---------------------|
| 1850–1860 | 27.8 years |
| 1880–1900 | 25.0 |
| 1920–1930 | 34.4 |
| 1940–1950 | 55.6 |
| 1950–1960 | 66.6 |

SOURCE: Reynolds Farley, *Growth of the Black Population* (Chicago, Ill.: 1970), 58–75.

1. What is the row variable? _____

2. What is the column variable? _____

3. What was the change in life expectancy for African-American women between 1850–1860 and 1880–1900? _____

4. Between 1900 and 1960? _____

5. Is the data in the table interval or nominal? _____

6. Does the variation in the life-expectancy data before and after the Civil War present any puzzle to you? _____

## Displaying Quantification: Graphs

The second basic type of quantitative display is the graph. The data in graphs can always be given in table form, but graphs are much more visually dramatic. There are three common types of graphs — the pie graph, the bar graph, and the line graph. The pie graph is a circle, with wedges representing the percentage each group or category contributes to the whole. A pie graph divides up the total evidence into its parts. Pie graphs are excellent for cross-sectional displays that show the distribution of a single variable at any one time. For example, pie graphs are often used to exhibit the proportion of the total vote that different political parties received in a given election year. Pie graphs may be used with nominal or interval data, but are most effective with nominal data. For example, if you wanted to show the percentage of people of different ethnic origins in the Unites States in 1860, you would use a pie graph. Figure 8.1 shows a sample pie graph.

Bar graphs show quantities. The extent, amount, or number of each category or group is represented by a rectangle whose base is the *x*-axis of a graph. The *y*-axis of the graph depicts the quantity. For example, a bar graph would be an excellent display of the differences in slave populations of various regions. Bar graphs can be used with interval or nominal data, but are usually chosen for interval-level data. Figure 8.2 shows a sample bar graph.

A line graph shows change in the data over time or compares the change in quantities against each other. A line graph begins with a scattergram, a plot of data points having an *x* and *y* coordinate. If the *x* coordinate is "time" — that is, a year or some other period of time — and the *y* coordinate is the measure of some variable — for example, the sale value of slaves in each of those time periods — the line

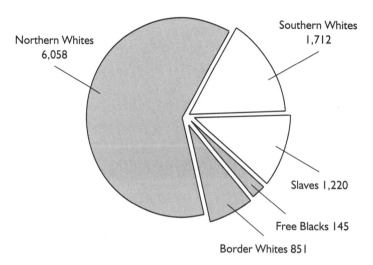

**FIGURE 8.1** *Population of Males 10 to 49 Years of Age in 1860 (in thousands)*

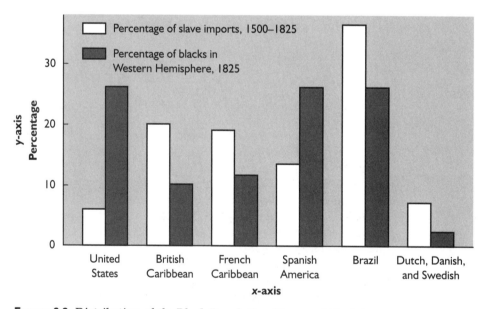

**FIGURE 8.2** *Distribution of the Black Population (Slave and Free) in 1825 Compared to the Distribution of Slave Imports, 1500–1825*

graph would show the change in the cost of buying a slave over time. Line graphs are commonly used to show increase and decrease of profits of a business, rates of interest, and other economic data. When such data is plotted against time, the time periods must be uniform. Any two variables that have some relationship to each other can be made into a line graph. Line graphs work best with interval data, but they can also be used to plot changes in nominal data over time. Figure 8.3 shows a sample line graph.

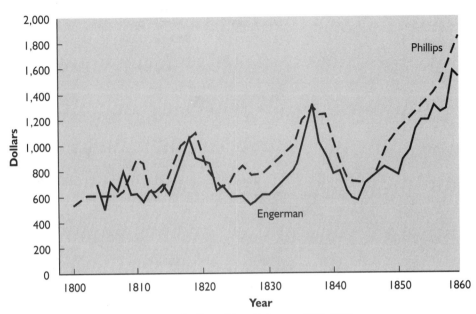

**FIGURE 8.3** *Price of a Prime Male Slave New Orleans, 1800–1860*

## EXERCISE 7: *Graphing Data*

The following data sets each lend themselves to only one kind of graph. Try your hand at turning them into the appropriate sort of graph. You may need to do some experimenting with rough sketches of different graphs to decide which type of graph best fits which data set. All data was taken from Bureau of the Census, *Historical Statistics of the United States* (1975), Part I.

| Data Set I | The Population of the South, 1800–1860 (in thousands of people) | | |
|---|---|---|---|
| 1800 | 2,622 | 1840 | 6,951 |
| 1810 | 3,461 | 1850 | 8,983 |
| 1820 | 4,419 | 1860 | 11,133 |
| 1830 | 5,708 | | |

Your graph for this data set should show how dramatically population in the South was rising throughout this period. Use the space below to draw your graph.

| Data Set 2  Southern Population, By Age Group, in 1860 (in thousands of people) | |
|---|---|
| Under 5 years old | 3,066 |
| 5–14 | 3,206 |
| 25–44 | 2,605 |
| 45–64 | 377 |
| Over 64 | 44 |

Your graph for this data set should highlight the fact that the population of the South was predominantly under the age of 45 on the eve of the Civil War.

| Data Set 3  Rural/Urban Population Distribution in the South, 1860 (in thousands of people) | |
|---|---|
| **Rural (percent)** | **Urban (percent)** |
| 10,791 (88%) | 1,497 (12%) |

This data set uses percentages. Does that suggest to you the type of graph that would best display the data?

## Numbers over Time

The change in cotton production from 1790 to 1860 was linear. On a line graph, the plotted data would resemble a straight line with an upward slope. Production grew very quickly and steadily, despite several periods when demand sharply fell and cotton prices suffered. If the table had included more time periods, these short depressions would have appeared in the table. By omitting them, the historian makes the growth of cotton export seem more regular.

On a graph, linear data may have a positive or a negative slope. See Figures 8.4(a) and (b). Inflation of prices for consumer goods is linear and positive, as is the rise in gross national product and population growth. Infant mortality rates and the size of families in modern societies are both linear and have a negative slope (meaning they decreased more or less steadily over time). Of course, the line is just an approximation of the actual distribution of the data. The line, like the words we use to describe what the line demonstrates — *increasing, growing, decreasing,* or *shrinking* — is just a device to depict a trend or direction of change over time.

Most historical changes are not linear at all, but come and go in cycles or even more complex patterns. If we were to graph such cyclical change — for example, the cycles of boom and bust that characterized the antebellum U.S. economy — our graph would look like the tracks on a roller coaster. See Figure 8.4(c). The antebellum economy, fueled by speculation over land and staple crops, was inherently unstable. Analytical historians have linked this instability with Americans' attitudes toward business and profits and connected political differences of opinion — for example, the difference of opinion over slavery between Northerners and Southerners on the eve of the Civil War — with the two regions' different responses to business cycles.

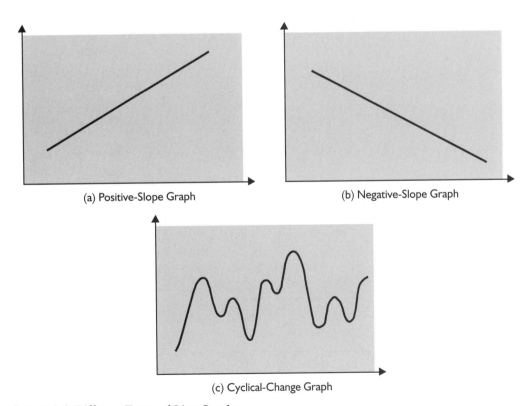

(a) Positive-Slope Graph

(b) Negative-Slope Graph

(c) Cyclical-Change Graph

**FIGURE 8.4** *Different Types of Line Graphs*

## EXERCISE 8: *Linear or Cyclical Change over Time?*

Following is another data set from the *Historical Statistics of the United States*. Plot the data points on the *x*- and *y*-axes in Figure 8.5, using the *x*-axis for years and the *y*-axis for prices. Connect the data points with lines, making a line graph. The index is a baseline figure that allows comparison of variations in actual prices over time. In this data set, the price of these goods in 1910 is the index. It is arbitrarily set to equal 100.

**Data Set 4 Wholesale Food Price, 1800–1847** (Index is price in 1910, set to = 100.)

| | | | | | | | |
|---|---|---|---|---|---|---|---|
| 1800 | 157 | 1812 | 141 | 1824 | 99 | 1836 | 128 |
| 1801 | 177 | 1813 | 172 | 1825 | 100 | 1837 | 132 |
| 1802 | 132 | 1814 | 181 | 1826 | 98 | 1838 | 128 |
| 1803 | 135 | 1815 | 187 | 1827 | 100 | 1839 | 126 |
| 1804 | 142 | 1816 | 172 | 1828 | 99 | 1840 | 102 |
| 1805 | 162 | 1817 | 184 | 1829 | 100 | 1841 | 90 |
| 1806 | 150 | 1818 | 172 | 1830 | 94 | 1842 | 80 |
| 1807 | 142 | 1819 | 140 | 1831 | 98 | 1843 | 77 |
| 1808 | 113 | 1820 | 109 | 1832 | 94 | 1844 | 72 |
| 1809 | 129 | 1821 | 102 | 1833 | 100 | 1845 | 84 |
| 1810 | 139 | 1822 | 109 | 1834 | 93 | 1846 | 96 |
| 1811 | 140 | 1823 | 108 | 1835 | 107 | 1847 | 87 |

Is the variable (wholesale food price) linear or cyclical? _____

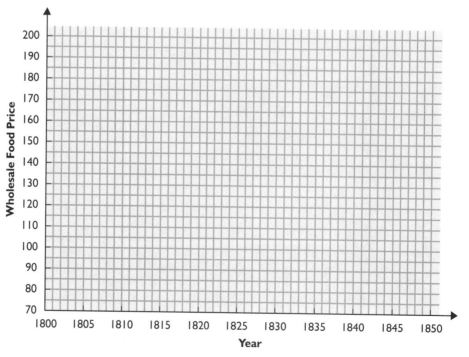

**FIGURE 8.5** *Wholesale Food Prices, 1800–1847*

# Patterns in the Past

Analytical historians seek patterns, regularities, and continuities in the past. An analytical study of southern planters' wives before the Civil War, for example, would begin by asking when these women married, how many children they had, what their place in the plantation economy was, and how they managed their household affairs. The analytical historian collects data to answer these and other questions about as many plantation wives as possible. The aggregation, or piling up, of individual cases is vital, for the analytical historian measures typicality and frequency. A single piece of evidence (for example, one of the letters mentioned in the first passage in exercise 3, might be quite moving but misleading. The analytical historian will not be content with anecdotal evidence, no matter how colorful or detailed it is.

Just as the authors of narratives arrange their facts in different ways, so analytical historians differ about the meaning of their evidence. Controversies among analytical historians often revolve about claims of typicality. When the analytical historian examines any single piece of evidence — one data point on a graph, one entry on a ledger, one piece of correspondence or diary entry — he or she asks whether that piece of evidence fits the larger pattern of evidence or is an exception to that pattern.

Over the past few decades, no subject in our early history has raised more controversy among analytical historians than the treatment of slaves in the pre–Civil War South. Deliberate brutality may have been rare — the typical master or mistress in the slaveholding states often had many close personal relationships with bondsmen and -women — but there is also much evidence of casual ill-treatment, that is, ill-treatment built into the system itself.

The most troubling of these systemic brutalities was the internal slave trade. The sale of husbands and wives away from each other and children away from parents disrupted slave families. Slave traders were busy entrepreneurs, and although some were regarded as "low-lifes," others were leaders in their community. The analytical questions that present themselves are: How central to the economy of the antebellum South was the slave trade? How often were slave families disrupted by the sale, gift, or bequeathal of one or more of their members? Did slave owners breed slaves for sale — giving inducements to young African-American slaves to bear children in order that they might later be sold?

## EXERCISE 9: *Evaluating Analytical Arguments*

There are many oral accounts of the breakup of slave families by slaves who escaped from bondage, were freed by their masters, or became free during and after the Civil War. These stories are deeply moving, but were the events they describe the rule or the exception? Analytical historical writing directly tackles the question of whether the events recalled in the slave narratives were typical or unusual.

The analysis of slave owners' participation in the slave trade in Robert Fogel and Stanley Engerman's *Time on the Cross* (1974) sparked a dispute that continues to this day over how analytical historians were to assess data on slave trading. Economists Fogel and Engerman sought to prove, using statistical analysis of plantation records and auctioneers' records, that few slave families were disrupted by the sale of their members. Following is an excerpt from Fogel and Engerman's proof, and a rebuttal by historians Herbert Gutman and Richard Sutch. There are questions after each selection for you to ponder.

**A** Abolitionists claimed that southern planters deliberately tried to "breed" slaves, as though African-American babies were a crop to be harvested and sold. Such breeding was never admitted by planters, but slaves were in fact sold. There was a slightly higher fertility rate of slave mothers in parts of the South whose land was no longer suitable for intensive agriculture. Abolitionists argued that instead of using their slaves to grow crops, planters in such parts of the South arranged for slave mothers to become pregnant more frequently. Fogel and Engerman deny this.

> The evidence put forward to support the contention of breeding for the market is meager indeed. . . . the evidence consists largely of unverified charges made by abolitionists and of certain demographic [population] data. However, subsequent corrections . . . have shown that rates of return on [money invested in male and female slaves] were approximately the same. And the many thousands of hours of research by professional historians into plantation records have failed to produce a single authenticated case of the "stud" plantations alleged in abolitionist literature . . . The demographic argument for the existence of slave breeding is based on two principal observations. First, the slave-exporting states [of Virginia and Maryland] had fewer slaves in the age group fifteen to twenty-nine, and more at very young and old ages, than the slave-importing states [in the deep South]. Second, the fertility rate, measured as the ratio of children under one year to women aged fifteen to forty-nine [the childbearing years] was slightly higher in the exporting than in the importing states. Neither of these demographic observations is sufficient to establish the existence of breeding for the market. The deviations of the age distribution in importing and exporting states existed not only for slaves but for free men. As such they are proof that both free men and slaves migrated from east to west. But this point has never been in contention. What is in contention is the claim that the slave migration took place through market trading [that is, slave selling] instead of through the migration of whole plantations . . . [even if slaves were bred for market, few were sold "down the river"]. Only 16 percent of the interregional movement of slaves took place through market trading. This small movement, an average of about twenty-five hundred persons per year [produced very little profit]. Indeed, one could more easily make a case for the indispensability of the sweet potato crop [to the economy of the South than the slave trade], since this item brought in more income to slaveowners than the interregional sale of their bondsmen.[5]

1. According to Fogel and Engerman, what motive drove all planters' behavior?

   _____

   _____

2. What two kinds of evidence do Fogel and Engerman consider? _____

   _____

3. How do they dismiss the first kind of evidence? _____

   _____

4. How do they handle the second kind? _____

   _____

5. What do they conclude? _____

   _____

6. Fogel and Engerman compared two different sets of figures on age distributions — slave *women* and free*men*. Might this inconsistency in any way weaken their argument? _____

_____

**B** Fogel and Engerman found strong critics in Herbert Gutman and Richard Sutch. Gutman and Sutch agreed that the profit motive was central to slavery but read the data on slave births in the upper South quite differently from Fogel and Engerman.

> The issue of slave breeding has been somewhat confused because participants in the debate have failed to define the term adequately. One of the present writers has defined it rather broadly as any practice of the slave master intended to cause the fertility of the slave population to be higher than it would have been in the absence of such interference. So defined, "breeding" includes the use of "rewards" for child-bearing, the encouragement of early marriage and short [breast-feeding] periods, and the provision of both pre- and post-natal medical care [for the mother and the infant], as well as practices more reprehensible to modern as well as to many nineteenth century sensibilities. . . .
>
> Whatever the definitions of "breeding," demographic evidence contained in the 1850 and 1860 censuses provides strong circumstantial evidence of the prevalence of inducements to childbearing, particularly in the so-called "breeding" states of the Atlantic seaboard and along the northern border of legal slavery. Slave women in these states exhibited higher fertility than did those of the importing regions, and their fertility rates approached the upper bounds of human capacity. . . .[6]

1. How do Gutman and Sutch define slave breeding? _____

_____

2. Have they in any way changed the Fogel and Engerman definition? _____

_____

3. If slave breeding is defined as any measure — including nutritious diets and medical care — that results in higher birthrate, could some slave masters have provided these benefits to pregnant slaves out of compassion, rather than out of a desire to breed and sell slave children for profit? _____

_____

4. What do Gutman and Sutch conclude about the meaning of elevated fertility rates in the upper South? _____

_____

5. Which argument do you find more convincing? Why? _____

_____

6. Think about the definitions of slave breeding and the question of what motivated slave masters to act as they did. Is 16 percent a small number of "interregional movement" of slaves, as they claim, or a large number of disruptions of family life? _____

_____

Fogel and Engerman and Gutman and Sutch transformed thousands of historical records listing individual slave sales into an exciting argument. Their grouping of data, use of numbers, and determination of patterns in the numbers would be quite convincing were it not for the fact that they thoroughly disagree with each other. They have employed highly sophisticated statistical tools to test the validity of their conclusions, and yet they remain as far apart in their conclusions as one can imagine. What are you to conclude?

Critics of analytical history would be quick to cite the controversy over slave breeding as proof that the entire enterprise of quantitative history is doomed to failure. Before you consent to this dismal conclusion, though, remember that narrative historians challenge one another's findings all the time. A more enlightened inference about analytical history from the controversy over slave breeding is that, in their efforts to discover the truth, the analytical historians have probed far more deeply into the subject than they could have without the tools of quantification. In the end, historical writing, with or without numbers, remains the creative act of human imagination — and such ventures will always lead to controversy.

Among the varieties of history, at the opposite end of the spectrum from analysis, is biography. As you will see in the next chapter, biographers are even more prone to controversy than analytical historians.

## NOTES

1. James Oakes, *The Ruling Race: A History of American Slaveholders* (New York: Vintage, 1982), 87.

2. Herbert G. Gutman, *The Black Family in Slavery and Freedom, 1750–1925* (New York: Pantheon, 1976), 92.

3. Kenneth S. Greenberg, *Masters and Statesmen: The Political Culture of American Slavery* (Baltimore: The Johns Hopkins University Press, 1985), 24.

4. Kenneth M. Stampp, *The Peculiar Institution: Slavery in the Ante-Bellum South* (New York: Alfred A. Knopf, 1956), 160–161.

5. Robert William Fogel and Stanley L. Engerman, *Time on the Cross, the Economics of American Negro Slavery* (Boston: Little, Brown, 1974), 1:78–86.

6. Gutman and Sutch, "Sexual Mores and Conduct" in Paul A. David, et al., *Reckoning with Slavery* (New York: Oxford University Press, 1976), 154–161.

# 9 BIOGRAPHY: LIFE AND TIMES

## Abraham Lincoln, Frederick Douglass, and Their Generation

Throughout his majestic *Decline and Fall of the Roman Empire* (1765), eighteenth-century English historian Edward Gibbon lamented that history was often little more than an organ of hatred or flattery. In his day and our own no branch of historical study is more prone to this vice than biography, the account of the thoughts and deeds of individuals. At the same time, there is no question that biography remains the most popular branch of historical writing.

## The Virtues and Vices of Biography

The sterling virtues of biography are obvious. Allan Nevins, one of the twentieth century's leading biographers, argued that the best biography should persuade the reader that the subject of the biography "lived, moved, spoke, and enjoyed a certain set of human attributes. We must not merely be shown what he did, but what he was, and why he was that kind of man."[1] Although Nevins wrote before most historians (women included) began to take the interest in women's history that has led to a virtual revolution in the practice of the historian's craft, his statement applies just as well to women as to men. Biography "humanizes the past,"[2] making it possible for us to relive a world otherwise strange to us.

Biography is one way of writing about history. The study of a person in a crucial moment in time can help anyone interested in the events and movements of that day understand why that person developed as he or she did. As Garrett Mattingly, the biographer of Catherine of Aragon, informed his readers, "Two things in her story have chiefly fascinated me: the way the decisions of a person by no means gifted with genius but strategically placed may influence the course of history, and the way that the divided loyalties common in thoughtful persons during a time of rapid change may affect their conduct in unexpected ways, and consequently give a twist, sometimes, to remote events."[3]

The vice lurking among the virtues of biography is that biographers may assign too great a role to their subjects, suggesting that all history depends on the whims or wiles of strategically placed people. This theory once dominated biographers' thinking. Thomas Carlyle, one of England's greatest biographers, insisted that great men were the makers of great events. Ralph Waldo Emerson, after reading Carlyle, concluded that all history is nothing more than biography. In a reaction to this oversimplified view of historical causation, later American and English historians retorted that the great man or woman was merely the spokesperson or the representative of great masses of people, speaking in a language that they understood and thereby moving them to action.

# Biographers and Biographies

Although one may debate the virtues and vices of biography, there is no question that good biography makes fascinating reading and opens up the past to us through the eyes of the biographer's subject. In an essay written shortly before she died, Barbara Tuchman explained that she wrote her Pulitzer Prize–winning biography of General Joseph Stilwell, U.S. military adviser in China during the Second World War, to help her readers understand American–Asian contacts. She used Stilwell as "a human vehicle" to carry her readers back to a critical period in the relations between the United States and its Asian friends and enemies. As she recounted Stilwell's trials and tribulations, Tuchman made America's experience in China "comprehensible to the reader."[4] In the end, the best biographers must strike a balance between seeing the past through the eyes of their subjects without letting the biases and aims of the subject distort the reader's view of the past.

Most biographers come to respect and like their subjects, appreciating the difficulties that their subjects faced and sharing the joys and sorrows their subjects experienced. For example, Nevins became the great defender of millionaire oil magnate John D. Rockefeller, a man much criticized by other scholars. Some biographers learn to dislike their subjects. Robert Caro, a biographer of the late President Lyndon Baines Johnson, admitted that "knowing Lyndon Baines Johnson — understanding the character of the thirty-sixth president of the United States — is essential to understanding the history of the United States in the twentieth century." Johnson was a great man whose decisions changed the course of history, and the broader outlines of his life illustrated "a panorama vast in scope: the panorama of the westward movement in America. . . ." Nevertheless, Caro concluded, "The more one follows his life, the more apparent it becomes that alongside the thread of achievement running through it runs another thread, as dark as the other is bright, and as fraught with consequences for history: a hunger for power in its most naked form, for power to . . . bend others to his will."[5] Of course, everyone, whether great or ordinary, has vices as well as virtues. The successful biographer enables the reader to see the virtues and vices of the subject from the inside, as though the reader knew the subject intimately.

## EXERCISE 1: *How Biographers See Their Subjects*

Different biographers often view the same person very differently; hence biography is the most subjective of all the forms of history. Biographers disagree about what sort of personality their common subject had and about how that person altered the course of history. Biographers even disagree about how their subject looked and sounded, as this exercise, based on biographies of Abraham Lincoln, illustrates. Read the excerpts from three biographies of Abraham Lincoln and answer the study questions about them.

"A. Lincoln," as he signed his name, remains one of the United States's most beloved presidents. His assassination at the end of the Civil War made him a martyr to the cause of the Union, but in life he revealed little of himself, even to his political allies. Asked to compose an autobiographical statement in December 1859 for the upcoming presidential campaign, he scribbled a few humorous lines about his "undistinguished family" and his meager schooling. He went on, "If any personal description of me is thought desireable, it may be said, I am, in height, six feet, four inches, nearly; lean in flesh, weighing, on an average, one hundred and eighty pounds; dark complexion, with coarse black hair, and grey eyes — no other marks or brands recollected."[6] Laconic, self-deprecating, protecting himself with humor — that was A. Lincoln. Here is how the biographers saw the man:

A. He looked like a farmer, it was often said; he seemed to have come from prairies and barns rather than city streets and barber shops; and in his own way he admitted and acknowledged it; he told voters from the stump that it was only a few years since he had worn buckskin breeches and they shrank in the rain and crept to his knees leaving the skin blue and bare. The very words that came off his lips in tangled important discussions among lawyers had a wilderness air and a log-cabin smack. The way he pronounced the word "idea" was more like "idee," the word "really" more like a drawled Kentucky "ra-a-ly." As he strode or shambled into a gathering of men, he stood out as a special figure for men to look at; it was a little as though he had come farther on harder roads . . . as though he had been where life is stripped to its naked facts and it would be useless for him to try to put on certain pretenses of civilization.[7]

1. Do you think that the biographer liked Lincoln? _____

2. From the passage you have read, do you think you would have liked Lincoln at first sight? _____

3. What about the biographer's technique caught your attention? _____

_____

4. In particular, does the biographer use common or colorful terms? _____

5. Do these terms capture Lincoln's own way of speaking? _____

B. As [Lincoln] cultivated the deceptively simple homespun stance of a stump speaker . . . so he also cultivated the artlessness of the circuit-riding storyteller. He would memorize those stories, walking around with clippings from newspapers or magazines or even with a comical book until he had them by heart and could slip them into conversations, interviews, or speeches on any occasion. . . . These stories had a practical, everyday value. As president, Lincoln used them to save time and temper. Under prodding from reporters, his secretary John Hay often tried to pry stories [out of Lincoln] for the sake of stories, but in the White House Lincoln listened. When he had to talk, stories helped keep that talk short, sweet, and to the point. . . .[8]

1. How does this biographer's approach to Lincoln differ from the approach in the first reading? _____

_____

2. Is it more cynical? less visual? more distant? less sympathetic? _____

_____

3. What does the biographer tell us about Lincoln's personality? _____

_____

C. Lincoln's renowned sense of humor was related to his passion for secrecy. Again and again self-important delegations would descend upon the White House, deliver themselves of ponderous utterances upon pressing issues of the war, and demand point-blank what the President proposed to do about their problems. Lincoln could say much in a few words when he chose, but he could also say nothing at great length when it was expedient. The petitioners' request, he would say, reminded him of "a little story," which he would proceed to tell in great detail, accompanied by mimicry and gestures, by hearty slapping of the thigh, by uproarious laughter at the end — at which time he would usher out his callers, baffled and confused by the smoke-screen of good humor, with their questions still unanswered.[9]

1. What is the difference between the Lincoln in excerpt C and the Lincoln in excerpt B? _____

_____

2. Does the biographer in excerpt C approach Lincoln from a new direction? care less for the man? see Lincoln as two men — one public and the other private?

_____

_____

## The Biographer's Imagination

How can biographers see the same person so differently? In Lincoln's case, perhaps the discrepancies can be attributed to his passion for secrecy and his self-lacerating sense of humor. Lincoln knew how to fabricate public masks and hide behind them, to bury inner feelings and project an image. The biographers' job is to go where their subjects' contemporaries could not go — into the subject's inner life. Biographers' views vary so widely because they express the biographers' own imaginative capacity to probe into the recesses of their subjects' lives. Visualize a model posing for a portrait by different artists — say Rembrandt, Goya, and Picasso. Would you not expect each portrait to look different? Biography is first and foremost an art form, and biographical portraits are works of art.

Biographers take primary sources and transform them, reshaping original words and pictures into new, more revealing words and pictures. For example, much of what we know about Abraham Lincoln's married life is based upon the recollections of the young man Lincoln took into his office in 1844, William Herndon.

Herndon was a complex man, about whose habits and abilities scholars disagree. In *A. Lincoln, Prairie Lawyer* (1960) John Duff opines that "the garrulous, windy, opinionated, prodigiously indiscrete Herndon, oracularly sure of himself and forever spouting dicta, was certainly not the happiest choice Lincoln could have made" as a partner in the law firm.[10] Historian David Donald believes that "there was something almost pathetic" in the way Herndon, a bright but unfocused man, sought knowledge.[11] A lawyer by trade, he was more of an intellectual than a working attorney and only his partnership with the more down-to-earth Lincoln ensured Herndon any regular income. Herndon did bring to the partnership political connections in the Whig party and growing commitment to radical reformism, including abolition of slavery. These commitments did not always sway the older Lincoln, but they influenced his thinking.

Herndon's *Life of Lincoln*, written (with the help of a young clerk, Jesse Weik) and published near the end of Herndon's life in 1889, is filled with opinion, unsubstantiated tales, and attacks on Lincoln's and Herndon's personal and political enemies. The modern editor of the work, Paul M. Angle, has decided that "confidence in his power of intuitive perception was, in fact, a dominant characteristic of William H. Herndon. Time after time he relied implicitly upon this faculty."[12] According to Angle, Herndon did not consciously lie about Lincoln, but he did treat his own hunches as though they were facts.

### EXERCISE 2: *How Biographers Use Sources*

In 1842, Lincoln married Mary Todd. Lincoln's parents were poor farmers; Todd's were well-to-do Kentucky slaveholders. A planter's daughter, Todd seemed an unlikely match for Lincoln. (See Figure 9.1.)

William Herndon and Mary Todd took an instant dislike to one another. Privately, Herndon spread rumors about Mary Todd's bad temper and Lincoln's prior and purer love for Ann Rutledge. After Lincoln's assassination, Herndon began to publicize his animosity for Mary Todd Lincoln, and she privately fumed, "'[It] will not be *well with* [*Herndon*] — if he makes the least disagreeable or false allusion in the future. He will be closely watched. W. H. [Herndon] may consider himself a ruined man, in attempting to disgrace others, the vials of wrath, will be poured upon his own head. . . .'"[13] Mary's biographer, Jean Baker, surmised, "No doubt Mary Lincoln remembered how the men of Lexington [Kentucky, where she was reared] had defended their lady loves with their swords and pistols . . ."[14] As you read Herndon's account, bear in mind the animosity between Herndon and Todd.

> That a lady as proud and as ambitious to exercise the rights of supremacy in society as Mary Todd should repent of her marriage to [Lincoln] surely need occasion no surprise in the mind of anyone. Both she and the man whose hand she accepted . . .

**FIGURE 9.1** *Abraham and Mary Todd Lincoln*

reaped the bitter harvest of conjugal infelicity. . . . Mrs Lincoln, on account of her peculiar nature, could not long retain a servant in her employ. The sea was never so placid but that a breeze would ruffle its waters. She loved show and attention, and if, when she gloried her family descent or indulged in one of her strange outbreaks, the servant could simulate absolute obsequiousness or had tact enough to encourage her social pretensions, Mrs. Lincoln was for the time her firmest friend. One servant . . . told me that . . . the secret of her ability to endure the eccentricities of her mistress . . . [was] that Mr. Lincoln gave her an extra dollar each week on condition that she would brave whatever storms might arise, and suffer whatever might befall her, without complaint. It was a rather severe condition, but she lived rigidly up to her part of the contract. The money was paid secretly and without the knowledge of Mrs. Lincoln.[15]

Biographers have regarded Herndon's views on Mary Todd Lincoln as a major, indispensable primary source on the life of Lincoln. Following are selections from three biographers based on Herndon's recollections. Each biographer gives Herndon's accusations a different twist. Answer the study questions after each passage.

A. Lincoln was indulgent as a father and left the upbringing of the children largely to "Mother," who was forebearing and overstrict by turns. Her whole nature took on a sort of instability as time went on. Devoted, even possessive toward her husband, she was eager to make him happy. But small matters upset her and brought on fits of temper. Servants found her difficult to please . . . Lincoln bore it all as best he could, taking her tongue lashings, yielding to her whims whenever possible, offering excuses to the neighbors, trying to make allowances for the affectionate wife and mother he knew she was at heart. When her upbraidings became unbearable he would not talk back or censure her, but simply slip off quietly to his office.[16]

How does the biographer balance criticism of Mary Todd, drawn from Herndon, with a more sympathetic view of Lincoln's wife?

_____

_____

_____


B. Mary's temper did not mellow with age. Neighbors, in time, adjusted to her loud, shrill voice, hysterical outbursts, and imagined fears. At the fierce explosions of anger everyone scurried for shelter. One after another, servants who resented her hectoring and felt exploited left; only those whom Lincoln secretly paid extra stayed. Mary indiscriminately scolded everyone around her, the children excepted, and on the slightest provocation flew into a fury, though once quieting down she tried to make amends.[17]

1. To what extent does this biographer rely on Herndon's view of Mary Todd?

_____

_____

_____

2. Is this account closer to Herndon's than the account in selection A? _____

_____

_____

C. Mary Lincoln's critics have held that her bad temper drove off her domestic workers, but such judgments remove her from her time and place. Everyone had difficulty keeping hired girls. In fact, the entire problem of finding and retaining good domestic help was a chronic concern for middle-class women. . . . Unlike the well-trained slaves of her childhood recollections, the independent daughters of Sangamon County's [Illinois] farmers required constant supervision in specific tasks such as the seasonal exigencies of housecleaning. Hired girls did not consider themselves servants, and they did not expect to be in service long. . . . Mary Lincoln on occasion did not have help because she refused to pay the market price, and it is her parsimony more than her bad temper that her employment [of servants] record reveals.[18]

1. Does this biographer credit or discredit Herndon's account? _____

_____

2. How does the author shift the reader's perspective by offering new information?

_____

_____

## EXERCISE 3: *The Interaction Between Biographer and Subject*

The biographer has a coworker in the transformation of a real life into a biography. The coworker is the subject herself or himself. All of us, during the course of our lives, think about where we have been, what we have done, and how others have seen us. In our letters, diaries, and recollections we not only rethink but remake our own lives, and such materials make possible a continuous interaction between the biographer and the subject, even if the subject is no longer alive.

You can explore the interaction between the subject's perception of himself or herself and the imagination of the biographer in the following excerpts from two versions of Frederick Douglass's autobiography, recalling his earliest youth. Douglass, seen in Figure 9.2, fled slavery in Maryland and became a leading abolitionist. During the Civil War he was Lincoln's adviser and emissary, though the two men did not always agree. Later, he served the United States as an ambassador. Douglass, passionate and dignified, wrote a series of autobiographies. The earliest, published in 1845, was short on personal details and long on analysis and condemnation of slavery. Extract A is taken from this volume. The second selection comes from the final version of his autobiography, published in 1892, shortly before he died. Why was there such a difference between the two accounts of the same events written by the same person? Specific questions and some points for you to ponder follow the two selections.

A. [1845] My mother and I were separated when I was but an infant — before I knew her as my mother. It is a common custom, in the part of Maryland from which I ran away, to part children from their mothers at a very early age. Frequently, before the child has reached its twelfth month, its mother is taken from it, and hired out on some farm a considerable distance off, and the child is placed under the care of an old woman, too old for field labor. For what this separation is done, I do not know, unless it be to hinder the development of the child's affection toward its mother, and to blunt and destroy the natural affection of the mother for the child. This is the inevitable result.[19]

B. [1892] Living thus with my grandmother, whose kindness and love stood in place of my mother's, it was some time before I knew myself to be a slave. I knew many other things before I knew that. Her little cabin had to me the attractions of a palace.

**FIGURE 9.2** *Frederick Douglass in 1855 and ca. 1885*

Its fence-railed floor — which was equally floor and bedstead — upstairs, and its clay floor downstairs, its dirt and straw chimney, and windowless sides, and that most curious piece of workmanship, the ladder stairway, and the hole so strangely dug in front of the fireplace, beneath which grandma placed the sweet potatoes, to keep them from frost in winter, were full of interest to my childish observation. . . . It was not long, however, before I began to learn the sad fact that this house of my childhood belonged not to my dear old grandmother, but to some one I had never seen, and who lived a great distance off. . . . called by grandmother, with every mark of reverence, "Old Master." Thus early did clouds and shadows begin to fall upon my path.[20]

Consider the differences in the two accounts. The first is didactic, as though part of a lecture on the evils of slavery. The second is more personal, sentimental, and self-revealing. Why did the first, written in 1845, when Douglass's memory of his childhood ought to have been fresh and detailed, give a much shorter description of his childhood in his grandmother's cabin than did the autobiography he wrote in 1892? Was the memory too hard to bear in 1845? Had it grown fonder with time by 1892? Or might Douglass have had a different purpose — a different face he wanted the public to see — in 1845 and 1892? Bear in mind that in 1845, Douglass was a leading abolitionist speaker and organizer throughout the Northeast.

---

---

---

---

## EXERCISE 4: *Biographers' Use of Autobiography*

Douglass's life has fascinated biographers. Not only had Douglass escaped from slavery to lead a rich and eventful life in the North, but he was a brilliant writer and public speaker as well. Douglass's autobiography has been the most important primary source for his biographers, but they have come away from the various versions of the autobiography with different impressions of its author. The following selections from three of his biographers concern the portions of the autobiographies you have already read. As you examine the passages, consider how the biographers have transformed Douglass's revelations about his early childhood. Questions follow each passage.

A. Frederick, as a small child, led a rather carefree life in his grandmother's cabin, but when he was about seven he felt for the first time the bitter reality of slavery.[21]

1. Which of Douglass's versions has the biographer adopted? _____

_____

2. How much space (and importance) does this biographer assign to Douglass's early childhood life? _____

_____

B. It was a happy time, one he would remember always as the most golden period of his life. He was as free as a bird; he could do anything he liked . . . As for Frederick, he was, in his own words, a "spirited, joyous, uproarious, and happy boy," without a care in the world. But gradually, as he grew older, the shape of things to come hove into hazy view. He learned that he was something called a *slave*, and that his grandmother and most of the others in his family were slaves also. There was a mysterious being, called "Old Master", who controlled their lives and who could make them all, even his grandmother, do anything he wanted them to do.[22]

1. What does this biographer emphasize in his account of Douglass's childhood?

_____

_____

2. Which version does he follow? _____

_____

C. Douglass wrote later of his boyhood in [his grandmother's] cabin as "spirited, joyous, uproarious, and happy," but drew a picture of the surrounding area that does not just reflect what he saw as a child. His description of the "worn-out sandy desert-like appearance of the soil," the "general dilapidation of its farms," and the "ague and fever" that rose from the Tuckahoe [plantation] is more a metaphor for the barrenness of slavery than the recollection of a six-year-old. It does, however, return attention from the idyllic to the realities of carving out a living in this remote country. . . . If the small house was indeed in the woods, as Douglass remembered it, the problem of providing food was immediate; you cannot grow vegetables under trees . . . In this realm [his grandmother] Betsy became legendary. Intelligent and physically powerful, she had made herself an expert in fishing and farming. . . . Douglass's stress on the impressive competence of his grandmother in what might have been thought of as masculine functions . . . is significant. . . . For the rest of his life Douglass looked to women as confidants, companions, and sources of strength. They rather than men could be . . . counted on. . . . They could also be the source of immense anguish.[23]

1. What new elements and perspectives does the third biographer introduce into the account? _____

_____

2. How close does he stay to Douglass's own words? _____

_____

3. How does he transform or penetrate what Douglass says to gain insights into the hidden, personal feelings of the man? _____

_____

# Writing Biography

We conclude this chapter with a short biographical assignment. Step one is to prepare a chronology. A biographical chronology is a time line on which you place important dates in your subject's life. These include events in which the person participated and events that were important to the person. The chronology should include both objective material (dates of birth, marriage, children's births, and information about occupation, education, public service, and military service) as well as subjective material (dates that the subject himself or herself regarded as important). The latter category might include meetings with other people, political events, travel, the reading of a particularly influential book or article, or similar moments in the subject's life. A chronology can be very detailed, but as with any historical writing, you must know what to omit as well as what to include. A chronology that is too detailed might have an entry for every day of the subject's life — surely too many entries for most biographies, although some biographers have approached this level of detail.

### EXERCISE 5: *Preparing a Chronology*

Choose a person — a parent or other close relative — with whose life you are quite familiar. Prepare on a separate sheet of paper a chronology of important objective and subjective dates in his or her life. You may interview your subject and ask for additional information from other family members. Seek information about education, employment, travel, and family matters. When you have finished a preliminary chronology, return to your sources and decide whether you have omitted any important episodes in your subject's life; if you have, include these. Your chronology should be about two pages long and resemble the following model:

    date #1    event
    date #2    event
    and so on . . .

### EXERCISE 6: *Life and Times, or Context*

Your chronology is only the skeleton of a life. The names and dates in it are bare bones until you put flesh on them by putting them into historical context. What was happening when your subject lived? Some of these events directly changed your subject's life or influenced your subject's thinking. Others were too remote to affect your subject. You must decide which contemporary events merit inclusion in your biography. Historical context is essential in a biography. Included in the immediate context is your subject's family, regional and ethnic background, his or her neighborhood, and the cultural (religious, ethnic, educational) and social circle in which he or she moved. Included in more general context are the political events and economic changes that shaped your subject's life.

Decide which national events and movements are important enough to merit treatment in your biography. What you include or omit is up to you. Examine the dates on your chronology. Using newspapers, the library, your textbook, and interviews with your subject, your subject's friends, relations, and coworkers (if possible), link those events or movements to the corresponding dates in your chronology. On a separate sheet of paper, write a paragraph associating each entry in your chronology with relevant outside events. For example, if your subject went to college between 1965 and 1969, you may decide to tie his or her experiences to the protests over the Vietnam War, the switch to open enrollment in many colleges, or increasing emphasis on science in the college curriculum in those years.

## EXERCISE 7: *The Inner Dimension of Biography*

The inner dimension of biography is your subject's feelings, ideas, and perceptions of the world. Biographers must assess their subject's thoughts and emotions empathetically. Seeing the world as the subject saw it is the most difficult and yet the most important task that a biographer can attempt.

Talk to your subject about his or her beliefs, ideas, and opinions. Determine how these relate to the important events in his or her life. If your subject is not available, attempt to gather information from those who knew your subject. To complete your biography exercise, select one issue or event that was important to your subject. Write a page on what your subject thought about that issue. Give evidence to support your interpretation of your subject's views. You may quote your subject, but you need not believe everything he or she says. Your subject's own words are primary sources and must be treated with the cautions described in Chapter 2.

The lives of Lincoln and Douglass came together in the Civil War. Lincoln asked Douglass to recruit African-American soldiers for the Union cause, and Douglass served with energy. At the same time, Douglass pleaded for equality for African-Americans, giving voice to a moral stance that was not popular among many political leaders of his day. For a time, Lincoln resisted the urging of Douglass and others to turn the Civil War into a struggle over equality, but reformers like Douglass continued to elevate the war effort into a struggle for the freedom of all peoples, and gave its terrible costs a moral dimension. They believed that history taught moral lessons and clung to that belief even when, after Reconstruction was abandoned, most other Americans turned their backs on the suffering of the freedmen and -women.

Was Douglass right? Does history teach us moral lessons? Can these lessons tutor future generations? In Chapter 10, we turn to these "big questions."

## NOTES

1. Allan Nevins, *The Gateway to History* (New York: Doubleday, 1962), 355.
2. Ibid., 348.
3. Garrett Mattingly, *Catherine of Aragon* (New York: Vintage, 1941), vii.
4. Barbara W. Tuchman, *Practicing History* (New York: Knopf, 1981), 65.

5. Robert A. Caro, *The Years of Lyndon Johnson: The Path to Power* (New York: Knopf, 1982), xvi, xvii, xix.

6. Abraham Lincoln, December 20, 1859, in Mario M. Cuomo and Harold Holzer, eds., *Lincoln on Democracy* (New York: HarperCollins, 1990), xlv, xlvi–xlvii.

7. Carl Sandburg, *Abraham Lincoln: The Prairie Years* (New York: Harcourt, 1926), 1:303–304.

8. P. M. Zall, "Abe Lincoln Laughing" in Gabor S. Boritt and Norman O. Forness, eds., *The Historian's Lincoln* (Urbana, Ill.: University of Illinois Press, 1988), 11–12.

9. David Donald, *Lincoln Reconsidered: Essays on the Civil War Era*, 2d. ed. (New York: Vintage, 1956), 67–68.

10. John J. Duff, *A. Lincoln: Prairie Lawyer* (New York: Holt, Rinehart & Winston, 1960), 97.

11. Donald, *Lincoln Reconsidered*, 39.

12. Paul M. Angle, ed., *Herndon's Life of Lincoln* (Greenwich, Conn.: Fawcett, 1961), 35.

13. Mary Todd Lincoln, November 1866, quoted in Jean Baker, *Mary Todd Lincoln: A Biography* (New York: W. W. Norton, 1987), 268.

14. Ibid., 269.

15. Angle, ed., *Herndon's Life of Lincoln*, 338–341.

16. Benjamin P. Thomas, *Abraham Lincoln* (New York: Knopf, 1952), 90–91.

17. Oscar Handlin and Lillian Handlin, *Abraham Lincoln and the Union* (Boston: Little, Brown, 1980), 86–87.

18. Baker, *Mary Todd Lincoln*, 106, 107.

19. Frederick Douglass, *Narrative of the Life of Frederick Douglass, An American Slave* (Boston, 1845), 2.

20. Frederick Douglass, *Life and Times of Frederick Douglass* [1892], ed. Rayford W. Logan (New York: Collier, 1962), 30–33.

21. Nathan Irvin Huggins, *Slave and Citizen: The Life of Frederick Douglass* (Boston: Little, Brown, 1980), 4.

22. Dickson J. Preston, *Young Frederick Douglass: The Maryland Years* (Baltimore: The Johns Hopkins University Press, 1980), 37–39.

23. William S. McFeely, *Frederick Douglass* (New York: W. W. Norton, 1991), 8, 9.

# $\bullet$10 BIG QUESTIONS: INEVITABILITY, MORALITY, AND THE LESSONS OF HISTORY

## *Civil War and Reconstruction*

Historians cannot avoid asking "big questions" — questions that go beyond what they have found in their sources. A big question may be compared to the shell of a nut. The meat of the nut is the historian's account, but the shell of the nut confines and shapes that account. Big questions may not be answerable, at least not through conventional means of narration, analysis, and biography, but they remind us of the complexity and significance of the historian's discipline. This chapter explores three of the big questions that shape every historical account: Are certain events inevitable? Is the historian permitted moral judgment? Can we learn from the past?

## Inevitability

First, the question of inevitability: was an event, a movement, or a development inevitable or could it have been avoided? For historians the question of inevitability begins with a simple query: we ask, If a certain person had acted differently, would the outcome of the story have been altered? This question is contrary to fact (after all, the person acted as he or she did), but the hypothetical "what if" focuses our attention on contingencies.

Contingencies are accidents or unplanned actions that can change the course of history. The classic example is the tale of the "want of a nail." For the want of a nail, a messenger's horse lost a shoe. Without the shoe, the horse went lame. Without the horse, the messenger was not able to deliver the message on time. Without the message, the general did not know where his enemy was, and his army was defeated.

The missing nail was a contingency, and history is filled with them. Harriet Beecher Stowe was not a general, but her dramatic tales of "Uncle Tom's Cabin," serialized in newspapers and then published in book form in 1852, galvanized antislavery opinion in the North. Would the Civil War have been fought had she not aroused the consciences of her readers? When Stowe visited Lincoln, early in 1863, he greeted her, "so you're the little woman who wrote the book that made this great war." If, for some reason, Stowe had never set pen to paper, would the Civil War have come when it did? or at all? Her decision to write *Uncle Tom's Cabin* was not a contingency, but its momentous impact on the debate over abolition of slavery could not have been foreseen — or could it? If the Civil War was inevitable, then the publication of *Uncle Tom's Cabin* was only one cause among many.

We can broaden our perspective on questions of contingency and inevitability by turning from individual actions to major events. We all ask ourselves whether wars could have been averted, plagues evaded, and people saved from the effects of their own folly. The ancient Greek Stoics, a group of philosophers who profoundly influenced Western thought, believed that all history was cyclical — it went around and around. In these cycles, nations rose, shone, decayed, and fell, to be replaced by other nations that would in their turn suffer the same fate. No people and no nation could escape from this unchangeable law of history. Eighteenth-century European and American Enlightenment leaders looked to the idea of progress for deliverance from these cycles of rise and decay. Through progress in science and technology and the spread of education, these thinkers argued, people could save themselves and their nations from ruin. Throughout the nineteenth century and into the first decade of the twentieth century, educated Americans and Europeans embraced this idea of progress. Having conquered much of the world and made great strides in science and the arts, Western peoples saw history in terms of one straight, upward motion. This line marked the decline of barbarism and the rise of Western civilization. Most Europeans ignored the baneful effects of imperialism.

In our own century, however, world wars, totalitarianism, and mass destruction of civilian populations gave pause to advocates of the theory of progress. Some historians, like Arnold Toynbee, went back to the Stoic ideal and warned about the rise and fall of Western civilization. Other scholars selected some period of the past as a golden age and extolled it over the present. Few historians still believe that progress is automatic. The simple faith of nineteenth-century historians in the inevitability of progress has vanished like a dream at morning.

## EXERCISE 1: *Was the Civil War Inevitable?*

Are great cataclysms inevitable? For example, could the Civil War have been delayed or averted? Did the division between the free North and the slave South make conflict irrepressible, as William Henry Seward told a meeting of voters in 1858, or could some compromise have been found, similar to the Missouri Compromise of 1820 or the Compromise of 1850? Read the following passages reflecting historians' opinions about the causes of the Civil War. After each, indicate whether the author thinks the Civil War was inevitable or avoidable. Explain your answer.

A. People fight under the stress of hyperemotionalism. When some compelling drive, whether it be ambition, fear, anger, or hunger, becomes supercharged, violence and bloodletting, thus far in human history, seem "inevitable." Now why was emotion in the United States in 1861 supercharged? . . . [there was] a deep seated enjoyment of political activity by Americans which proved dangerous. They gave themselves so many opportunities to gratify their desire for this sport. There were so many elections and such constant agitation . . . A great disruptive fact was the baneful influence of . . . [political] campaigns never over, and of political uproar endlessly arousing emotions. . . . This constant agitation certainly furnishes one of the primary clues to why the war came. It raised to ever higher pitch the passion-rousing oratory of rivals. They egged one another on to make more and more exaggerated statements to a people pervasively . . . isolated and confused.[1]

_____

_____

_____

B. The Abolitionists now felt themselves carried along by the tide of events and urged and pushed Lincoln [not to compromise]. But the moderates and the doubters were a powerful party for all that. The accusation of the South, describing Lincoln as the despot trying by brute force of arms to do violence to free American states, found echoes in the Northern [Democratic] press and in the Congress . . . But why go on piling up instances and particulars? I am quite ready to concede the point. The American people had suddenly found themselves in the Civil War and the majority in none of the sections [of the country] had deliberately willed it. . . . Does it prove that the war might therefore have been avoided? Is it not rather one more proof of the general truth that the course of history is not governed by the conscious will of the majority?[2]

_____

_____

_____

C. Had the economic systems of the North and the South remained static or changed slowly . . . the balance of power [in the federal government] might have been maintained indefinitely by repeating the [compromise] . . . tactics of 1787, 1820, 1833, and 1850 . . . But nothing was stable in the economy of the United States or in the moral sentiments associated with its diversities. Within each section of the country, the necessities of the productive system were generating portentous results. . . . shifting with mechanical precision the weights which statesmen had to adjust in their efforts to maintain the . . . peace [between North and South].[3]

_____

_____

_____

D. War causation tends to be "explained" in terms of great forces. Something elemental is supposed to be at work, be it nationalism, race conflict, or quest for economic advantage. With these forces predicated, the move toward war is alleged to be understandable, to be "explained" and therefore to be in some sense reasonable. [but] Warmaking is too much dignified if it is told in terms of broad national urges . . . or of compelling . . . ambitions. When nations stumble into war, or when peoples rub their eyes and find they have been dragged into war, there is at some point a psychopathic case. Omit the element of abnormality, of bogus leadership . . . and diagnosis [of the causes of war] fails.[4]

_____

_____

_____

**EXERCISE 2:** *Identifying Turning Points in History*

It is easy from a distance, writing in generalities, to take sides on the question of the inevitability of the Civil War. It is not nearly so easy to rewrite the history of the days and weeks before the first shot was fired on the Union garrison at Fort Sumter in the harbor of Charleston, South Carolina. Were there moments in time when a different decision might have changed the course of history?

The following series of passages traces the crisis at Fort Sumter in the winter and spring of 1861. If the cast of characters — soldiers on both sides, Governor Francis W. Pickens of South Carolina, President-elect Lincoln, and their many advisers — need not have acted as they did, how might they have acted? After each paragraph, write in the space provided what the key decision was and how the decision might have been different. Be historically minded in your approach to the exercise: How did the actual participants see themselves and their plight? Did white Southerners fear that their slaves would be taken from them and, perhaps worse, freed in their midst? Would the president and his newly victorious Republican party give up the spoils of their victory or give in on their campaign promise to stem the advance of slavery?

A. However much the border South wished to avoid a confrontation between [the North and South], by April of 1861 both Jefferson Davis [President of the Confederate States of America] and Abraham Lincoln had good reason to seek one. Neither president wanted war, but both had to have an end to the ambiguity surrounding the secession crisis. During his first month [of March] in office Lincoln could afford to stall. He needed to form his administration, he hoped that the great mass of Southern whites would "come to their senses," and he sought support for the Union among the border states. Davis, too, required time to construct his government and to proselytize [for support] among the slave states still in the Union. By April, though, both governments had done what they could about the border South; people and governments on both sides had begun to clamor for decisive action.

1. What key decisions lay before Lincoln? _____

_____

2. What crucial decisions did Davis have to make? _____

_____

B. At [Fort] Sumter [in the harbor of Charleston, S.C.] the situation had become critical. Major Anderson [commander of the Union garrison at the fort] and his garrison were running out of food. Women and children, dependents of the troops, left the fort in early February; but even without the extra mouths to feed, Anderson calculated that he would be starved out before mid-April. To retain Sumter the United States would have to send in supplies. To be rid of the Union presence in Charleston Harbor the Confederacy would then be compelled to open fire on the resupply ship or the fort or both. Both sides accepted the confrontation then and there.

1. What problems did Major Anderson face? _____

_____

2. How might he have resolved them? _____

_____

3. What were Lincoln's choices now? _____

_____

C. On April 7 a federal fleet sailed for Charleston to resupply Anderson's garrison. A day later the Confederate commissioners in Washington received a letter, dated March 15 but held back by [new secretary of state William Henry] Seward, stating that the United States had no intention of abandoning Sumter. The same day, April 8, Robert Chew of the United States State Department arrived in Charleston and personally read a message from his President to Governor Pickens [of South Carolina] which explained that Lincoln planned to send provisions to Fort Sumter but would not send more troops or arms. After Pickens had heard his tidings, Chew left in some haste.

1. What decision had Lincoln made? _____

_____

2. How had he presented the decision to Governor Pickens? _____

_____

3. How might Lincoln have acted differently? _____

_____

D. Pickens promptly relayed Lincoln's message to the Confederate military commander at Charleston, General P. G. T. Beauregard, who passed the news on to his commander in chief in Montgomery [Alabama, still the capital of the confederacy]. Then it was Davis's turn to act. All along he had believed that war was inevitable, and although he did not wish to fire the first shot, he perceived no alternative. Accordingly, on the tenth [of April, his] secretary of War Walker sent orders by telegraph to Beauregard to demand evacuation [of Sumter] and to reduce [by force] the fort should the demand be refused.

1. What options did Davis have when Pickens informed Davis of Lincoln's plan?

_____

_____

2. How did Davis respond? _____

_____

E. At two o'clock on the afternoon of April 11, Beauregard sent a written demand to Anderson. Two of the General's aides, Colonel James Chesnut and Captain Stephen D. Lee, presented the note to Anderson with appropriate formality. No one involved in the Sumter confrontation missed the drama and import of what was happening. Beneath the courtesy and fastidious propriety of the proceedings, however, were the hard facts that Anderson refused to move and Beauregard meant to move him.[5]

1. Did Beauregard have any choice but to behave as he did? _____

_____

2. Did Anderson have any choice? _____

_____

3. How might they have averted actual conflict, if they so chose? _____

_____

# Moral Responsibility

In the previous exercise, you discovered that even for men and women who believe in free will, some choices do not come easily. The choice between honor and autonomy, on the one hand, and the prospect of war on the other, was not one that southern leaders or northern politicians welcomed. The extreme case of this dilemma is not uncommon in history: a person coming to believe that what appears to be a choice is no choice at all. Every road leads to the same ending place. Is the resulting series of events then inevitable? In this sense, the coming of the Civil War was a tragedy that many foresaw but none seemed able to prevent. Does this apparent paradox mean that no one bore any moral responsibility for the one million casualties — dead, wounded, and missing — and the billions of dollars of damage to homes and workplaces? Is such responsibility justified by the emancipation of four million people held in perpetual bondage?

In the twentieth century, the question of moral responsibility — and moral judgment — has become a second big question for historians. After so many human cataclysms — Adolf Hitler's attempt to destroy European Jewry; Stalin's atrocities in the Soviet Union, Japanese militarists' experiments with chemical and germ warfare, American aerial assaults on Japanese population centers, and countless other cases of barbarous conduct by "civilized" governments — questions of guilt have become inescapable historical issues. May the historian assign blame?

All writing, historical and otherwise, is filled with implicit moral judgment. The words we choose can never be wholly neutral, nor do we want them to be. To persuade and inform readers, history must touch moral sensibilities. Without some judgment of their subjects' actions, historians' writing would simply disintegrate like a mummified parchment unwrapped in the sunlight. At the same time, historians do not want to patronize or override the moral belief systems of their subjects. This would violate the basic tenets of historical-mindedness — to see the past through the eyes of the people who lived then.

Can one escape from the dilemma by asserting that there is one moral code that all Americans, past and present, share, and then use this code to judge Americans' conduct in the past? Historians have written volumes about Americans' belief in liberty, opportunity, and equal protection of law. These words capture moral ideals celebrated in our politics and written into our laws, but have the words always been translated into real liberty, opportunity, and equal protection? If we look at the treatment of women and certain minorities — for example, Native Americans, Irish, Eastern European, and Asian immigrants, and African-Americans — over much of our history, would we find evidence that those ideals were embedded in reality? If we cannot find such proof, must we then conclude that moral pronouncements so prominent in our legal and political speech are either self-delusions or deliberate lies? If so, can historians presume to substitute their own modern moral sensitivities for the moral values of the people they are studying?

## EXERCISE 3: *Identifying Moral Judgment in Historical Accounts*

The era of Reconstruction has raised as many moral questions as any period in our history. In this exercise, excerpts from historians' accounts of Reconstruction demonstrate a variety of moral judgments, both implicit and explicit. Look for the historians' words implying a moral stance in each passage, and answer the questions at the end of each.

**A** President Lincoln's successor, President Andrew Johnson, began reconstruction of the Confederate states immediately after the close of hostilities, allowing former Confederate leaders and soldiers to swear loyalty to the Union and alter their states' constitutions to forbid slavery. The governments of these "presidentially reconstructed" southern states then wrote "Black Codes" that denied to former slaves full equality under law.

> In effect, the Black Codes made all Negroes free but not equal to whites in civil rights, made the ex-slaves roughly equivalent to the free Negroes of slave times . . . the Black Codes created a class of Americans excluded by law because of race and color from the capacity to protect itself in courts equally with whites through testimony, to be fully responsible for marketplace decisions, or to live without fear of prejudiced application of criminal justice. . . . the notorious vagrancy and apprentice clauses commonly placed unemployed and minor [underage] blacks whose parents lacked funds under white employers' control, and permitted employers to exercise penal [criminal-law] authority.[6]

1. What key words or phrases signal to you these authors' moral stance? _____

   _____

2. What is the authors' opinion of the Black Codes? _____

   _____

**B** Recoiling at reports of the ill-treatment of former slaves under the Black Codes and equally worried that the Republican party would gain few votes in the South if former slaves and unionists were not supported by the federal government, the Republicans in Congress took charge of Reconstruction. Here are two historians' opposing views of the new turn of events.

> Even when the former confederates were rather firmly in control of Southern state and local governments in the early postwar years, violence was an important part of the pattern of life. In 1866 the head of the [federal] Freedman's Bureau [to help former slaves] in Georgia complained that numerous bands of [white] ruffians were committing "the most fiendish and diabolical outrages" on the freedmen. The former slaves themselves made many representations to Congress and the President that they were in constant danger of physical harm at the hands of the former Confederates. Northern teachers of freedmen frequently saw their efforts literally turn to ashes as local white opponents set fire to the Negro schools . . . If violence was an integral part of the old order and even of the new order controlled by former Confederates, it was only natural that it would be a prime factor in any move to oppose the still newer order administered by those whom the former Confederates regarded as natural enemies [from the North].[7]

1. With what words or phrases does this author identify for us his approval or

   disapproval of the former Confederates? _____

   _____

   of the agents of the Freedman's Bureau? _____

   _____

   of the purposes of Reconstruction? _____

   _____

> In the autumn of 1866 and through the winter and summer of 1867 strange men from the North were flocking into the black belt of the South, and mingling familiarly with

the negroes, day and night. These were the emissaries of the Union League Clubs . . . Organized in the dark days of the war to revive the failing spirit of the [northern] people, they had become bitterly partisan clubs with the conclusion of the struggle, and, the Union saved, they had turned with zest to the congenial task of working out the salvation of their [Republican] party. This, they thought, depended on the domination of the South through the negro vote. Sagacious politicians, and men of material means, obsessed with ideas as extreme as those of [the radical Republicans] they dispatched agents to turn the negroes against the Southern whites and organize them in secret clubs. Left to themselves, the negroes would have turned for leadership to the native southern whites [their former masters] who understood them best. This was the danger. [It was] imperative, then, that [the negroes] should be taught to hate — [the white southerners] . . . Over the plantations these [Union League] agents wandered, seeking the negroes in their cabins, and halting them at their labors in the fields, and the simple-minded freedmen were easy victims of their guile.[8]

1. What words or phrases reveal this author's view of southern whites? _____

_____

   of freedmen and -women? _____

_____

   of Union League agents? _____

_____

2. What is his opinion of Republican political recruiting in the South? _____

_____

   **C** The "Reconstruction Amendments" to the United States Constitution (the Thirteenth, Fourteenth, and Fifteenth Amendments) ended slavery, told state governments they must afford equal protection under the law to all persons, and barred discrimination in voting on the basis of race. A series of Civil Rights Acts from 1866 through 1875 gave teeth to these amendments. Former slaves and free African-Americans were soon taking on important posts in the congressionally reconstructed governments.

> The Negroes were seldom vindictive in their use of political power or in their attitude toward native whites. To be sure, there were plenty of cases of friction between Negroes and whites, and Negro militiamen were sometimes inordinately aggressive. But in no southern state did any responsible Negro leader, or any substantial Negro group, attempt to get complete political control into the hands of the freedmen. All they asked for was equal political rights and equality before the law. . . . Negroes did not desire to have political parties divided along racial lines; rather, unlike most white Democrats, they were eager to drop the race issue and work with the whites within the existing party framework.[9]

1. With what words or phrases does this author express his view of Negro conduct in the Reconstruction era? _____

_____

2. What is his moral stance on Reconstruction? _____

_____

**D** The best hopes of the Republican reconstruction governments were dashed and the worst fears of their Democratic opponents were confirmed when many of the economic projects designed to put the South on its feet again crashed down in bankruptcy. Corruption, widespread throughout the United States, had an especially disheartening effect in the South, according to the author of the next passage.

> Corruption through bribery and extortion had brought great damage to the railroads [planned and built in the South by the new governments]; yet this form of corruption was the least important kind. If the term is broadened to include other, more subtle betrayals of the public interest, "corruption" involved almost every man and measure of the Reconstruction period. Many corporations did not deserve [government] aid. A systematic railroad policy could not endow all lines equally. Yet the legislature gave support to undeserving roads, not because the projects seemed good, but because the representatives, blinded by local prejudices and impractical visions, allowed themselves to place local gain above sectional and state good. State pride corrupted legislators. . . . selfishness, in all its forms, made the railroad aid programs a jumble of different subsidies and encrusted the financial burdens on taxpayers. Here was the real corruption. . . . not only a corruption of ethics, but a corruption of judgment. The latter was by far the more serious of the two.[10]

1. With what words and phrases does this author convey moral messages?

   _____

   _____

2. What is his final judgment on Reconstruction? _____

   _____

   _____

# The Lessons of History

Beneath the historians' disparate views of Reconstruction, embedded in explicit and implicit judgments, were the authors' moral visions. For some of these historians, Reconstruction was a tragedy because it burdened the former Confederates with military occupation and political subjugation or because it never fulfilled the ideals of equality under law or racial fair play. Historians writing about Reconstruction cannot help expressing their moral judgment; their language, like all language, is inherently moralistic and no author can escape its constraints.

If even the most conscientious and fair-minded historian cannot help but engage in implicit moral judgment, few historians have been so explicit or so bold as Howard Zinn, who wrote: "I start, therefore, from the idea of writing history in such a way as to extend human sensibilities, not out of this book into other books, but into the going conflict over how people shall live, and whether they shall live."[11]

A third big question that preoccupies not only historians but everyone who takes the study of history seriously is, Does history teach lessons we can use today and tomorrow? The philosopher Georges Santayana wrote that those who forgot history were fated to relive it. In his day, this applied to the makers of World War I, who, after nearly a century of peace, disregarded what great wars did to nations. Yet a mere generation after the Great War, Europeans were again locked in mortal combat. It is easy to see the differences between the First and Second World Wars, but we can still wonder whether the makers of World War II misread the lessons of history. Adolf Hitler had seen firsthand the horrors of the First World War — he served in the German army on the western front and was wounded in the last year of the war — yet he drew from history the lesson that Germany should avenge a bitter defeat rather than pursue peace. To the leaders of England and France, the Great War had taught other lessons and blinded by these, they failed to realize the threat that Hitler posed to peace. It is tempting to agree with historian Martin Duberman that the only lesson history teaches is that there are no lessons, only "bitter disappointment" for those interested in "changing the present" through knowledge of the past.[12]

However real our fears may be that political leaders never learn lessons from history, modern policy makers and social scientists still desire to use the past to help governments avoid repeating disastrous mistakes. *Thinking in Time*, the title of Ernest May and Richard Neustadt's attempt to raise the "historical conscious-ness" of our political leaders, suggests that such an endeavor is urgently needed. They conclude that a study of the past, even the brief one allowed to busy policy makers (not unlike the brief time you can give to history in your crowded class schedule and your hectic days at school) can be valuable if our leaders ask the question, What would a little more study, a little broader study, gain? It is remark-able how much more accurate our predictions about the present and the future would be if we were to take just one more step into the past.[13]

You may well ask, if the task of predicting the future from the past is possible, why have wise and well-informed leaders so often — almost regularly — led their peoples into disaster? The answer may be that history — like weather storms or the disruptions of motion in fluids — is dependent on small differences, variations of individual action so minute, so easily lost in the welter of mass movements, that they are not easily perceived at the time, much less recovered by later scholars. These minute variations in the initial conditions of two otherwise apparently similar events may produce, at the end of a long chain of human actions and responses, very different outcomes. Physicists call this "the butterfly effect" — the theory that the wind currents that a butterfly in Georgia creates will affect the weather in London, England. Were the butterfly resting the next day and all else the same, the weather would be different in London, for minute variations will have wider and wider effects until they change the world in which we live. Thus we return to the first theme of this chapter, "for want of a nail."

## EXERCISE 4: *Learning from the Past*

The last exercise in this book, like the first exercise in Chapter 1, requires you to think rather than write. Reviewing in your mind the materials on American history you have studied this term, ask yourself what lessons in our past may point the way to a better future. For example, can you apply what you have learned about race relations to today's debate over minority rights? How does your knowledge of that part of our past help you to predict what will happen in the future of race relations? Is future conflict inevitable? Can compromises be found that make every-one a winner? Or must there always be victors and vanquished? Think about it.

Much of what you have learned this term would serve well those who decide our nation's fate. Perhaps, if you find yourself in that role, you will use the skills that you have mastered to prove May and Neustadt right. Bear in mind, however, that the human past is not recaptured in straight lines or in easy-to-solve formulas of economic or political interaction. Like nature itself, human history is the "rough, not rounded, scabrous, not smooth . . . pitted, pocked, and broken up, the twisted, tangled, and intertwined" expression of the human condition.[14]

## NOTES

1. Roy Franklin Nichols, *The Disruption of American Democracy* (New York: Macmillan, 1961), 502–504.
2. Pietr Geyl, *Debates with Historians* (New York: Meridian, 1958), 249–250.
3. Charles Beard and Mary Beard, *The Rise of American Civilization* (New York: Macmillan, 1927), 2:3–4.
4. James G. Randall, "A Blundering Generation," in *Lincoln the Liberal Statesman* (New York: Dodd, Mead, 1947), 36–64.
5. From *The Confederate Nation* by Emory M. Thomas, excerpted from pp. 67–92. Copyright © 1979 by Emory M. Thomas. Reprinted by permission of HarperCollins Publishers.
6. Harold M. Hyman and William M. Wiecek, *Equal Justice Under Law: Constitutional Development, 1835–1875* (New York: Harper & Row, 1982), 320.
7. John Hope Franklin, *Reconstruction After the Civil War* (Chicago: University of Chicago Press, 1961), 152–153.
8. Claude G. Bowers, *The Tragic Era: America After Lincoln, The Dark That Followed the Dawn of Peace* [1929] (Cambridge, Mass.: Houghton Mifflin, 1962), 198.
9. Kenneth M. Stampp, *The Era of Reconstruction, 1865–1877* (New York: Knopf, 1966), 168–169.
10. Mark W. Summers, *Railroads, Reconstruction, and the Gospel of Prosperity: Aid Under the Radical Republicans, 1865–1877* (Princeton: Princeton University Press, 1984), 116–117.
11. Howard Zinn, *The Politics of History* (Boston: Beacon Press, 1970), 35–36.
12. Martin Duberman, *The Uncompleted Past* (New York: E. P. Dutton, 1971), 356.
13. Richard E. Neustadt and Ernest R. May, *Thinking in Time: The Uses of History for Decision Makers* (New York: Free Press, 1986), 232–246.
14. James Gleick, *Chaos: Making a New Science* (New York: Viking, 1987), 94.